PARABLES *and* PARADOX

The Offensive Gospel

STEPHEN HARRISON AND
RICHARD HUIZINGA

ISBN 978-1-956001-71-6 (paperback)
ISBN 978-1-956001-72-3 (eBook)

Copyright © 2021 by Stephen Harrison and Richard Huizinga

All rights reserved. No part of this publication may be reproduced, distributed, or transmitted in any form or by any means, including photocopying, recording, or other electronic or mechanical methods without the prior written permission of the publisher.

Printed in the United States of America

Offensive: two meanings

a. To offend, insult
b. To challenge, to move against, to conquer by a superior action

This Book is dedicated to our wives Marilyn Harrison and Shari Huizinga.

Contents

Preface 1

Introduction 3
   The Offensive Gospel 3
   The Hopefully Inoffensive Gospel 5
   Symbols 7
   Humor 9
   Between 2 Parables 10

Chapter 1 – Identity 13
   Humble Birth 13
   Jesus Birth to the Disciples 13
   Matthew Advent 15
   Mark Advent 16
   John Advent 17
   Luke Humor and Advent Part 1 18
   Humor in Luke's Advent Part 2 19
   I am statements in John part 1 21
   Redemption Circle – The Not So Missing Link 23
   I Am statements – As Metaphors 25
   John and Metaphors part 1 26
   John Metaphors part 2 28
   John Metaphors part 3 29
   I Am Statements – The Future Revealed 31
   Recognizing the Messiah 32

Recognizing the Messiah – Other Encounters 34
Rabbi Jesus..36
Rabbi Jesus and the Disciples 38
Some Concluding Observations On Rabbi....................40
Who Do People Say That I Am Versus What I Am 41
Who Do People Say That I Am – Closing Question................43

Chapter 2 – Sermon On The Mount & Other Basics........................45
Sermon on Truth...45
Sermon on Anger 46
Sermon on Transparency 48
Sermon on Priorities..49
Sermon on Wisdom 49
Sermon on Priorities (The Challenge of Being Human) 51
The Lord's Prayer 52
The Ego and The Lord's Prayer 54
Cost Value Options 55
God and Ambiguity 57
Simple Prayers...58
Sermon on The Mount Introductory Commands...........59
Sermon on The Mount – Be Authentic 61
Sermon on The Mount – The Golden Rule....................63
Being And Doing 64
Social Justice and The Sermon on the Mount................65
A Higher Law From the Sermon on the Mount.............67
Social Justice and the Sermon on the Mount Practical Advice.....68
Prosperity And The Sermon On The Mount Part One.............70
Prosperity And The Sermon On The Mount Part 2..................71

Chapter 3 – The Really Offensive Gospel...74
Prelude and overview of the Major Offenses..................74
Parable of the Talents..77
Parable of the Vineyard 78
Vineyard Fairness 81

Shrewd Manager 82
Family Offense 84
Rich Fool Part 1 85
The Rich Man, Creation, and The Ego 86
The Unjust Judge 89
Mountains, Mustard Seeds, and Perverts 89
The Prodigal 91
Jesus Sweats Blood 94
The Cross as Mystery 96
Mystery in the New Testament 97

Chapter 4 – Temptation 99
Temptation like Jesus 99
Going Deeper into Temptation 100
Temptation Revisited 102
The mission 103
The Not So Unreasonable Temptations of Jesus 104
Struggling With Temptation 105
When Peter Tempted Jesus 108
Little Children 109
Tempting Jesus From Satan to His Best Friend and Beyond 110
When Jesus followed Satan 112
The Temptations of Jesus and the Seven Deadly Sins 114

Chapter 5 – Forgiveness 117
Subject: The Birth of Forgiveness 117
The Unforgiving Servant 119
Brother Anger Paradox 120
Mercy and the Unforgiving Servant 121
Forgiveness and Love 123
Forgiveness Formula 125
Why Judas Hung Himself 127
Who Really is Forgiven in the Prodigal 130
Universal Emotions and Reconciliation 131

  Fatted Calf 134
  Metaphors in John and The Gift of Forgiveness 135

Chapter 6 – Inclusion 139
  Inclusion 139
  Mark's Perspective 140
  Good Samaritan 144
  Specific Healings 146
  Healings and Strange Proclamations 148
  Parable of the Sower: Jesus' most Basic Parable 151
  Nicodemus 153
  Do You Love Me Simon Peter? 154
  Rich Young Ruler Parable or Real Life 156
  Rich Young Ruler's True Identity 157
  Eternal life 159
  Between Criminals 161
  A Wide Net 162

Chapter 7 – Women 164
  Healing Women 164
  True Healing 165
  Mary, Martha 167
  Washing Jesus Feet 169
  Woman Caught in Adultery 170
  Jesus Solicits a Woman of Ill Repute 172
  Washing Feet and Giving Thanks, His Mission and the
    Cost of Discipleship 174
  Women in High and Low Places 177
  Women Uplifted 178
  Parable Gender Part 1 180
  Parable Gender Part 2 182
  Parable Gender Part 3 184

Chapter 8 – Prodigal 189
   Prodigal Disclaimer 189
   A Father's Early Pain on Departure 189
   The Prodigal Comes to His Senses 190
   Before Coming to His Senses 191
   Image Distraction 192
   Compassion 192
   Hunger 194
   Entitlement 195
   The Robe 195
   Ownership, or Grace, or Works? 197
   Quick, Safe and Sound 198
   Endless Anger 199
   What's in a Name 200
   Jealousy 201
   The Confession 202
   The Suppressed Confession 203
   Home 205
   A Father Pleads 206
   Suffering, Compassion, and Reconnection 207
   Free Will and the Prodigal 208
   Surprise 209
   Ten Commandments 210
   Who is Sought 210
   Prodigal Atonement Part 1 212
   Prodigal Atonement Part 2 Justice or Inclusion 213

Chapter 9 – Jesus Christ Superstar And The Gospel As Symphony 216
   Jesus Christ Superstar as Both Unorthodox and Paradox 216
   Jesus Christ Superstar II 217
   Jesus Christ Superstar III 219
   Superstar John 19:41 221
   Who Saw Jesus First After the Resurrection 223

Resurrection Beings 224
Why Do You Seek The Living Among The Dead 228
The Gospel for Modern Times 230
Gospel As A Symphony 233

Conclusion 237
Two Parables as a Gospel Summary 237
Cost of Discipleship 238
Jesus on The Essentials 239
I Am Who I Was 241
The Offensive Gosepl Matthew 25 243
Interjection 245
Righteousness 245
Sacrifice or Skin in the Game 247
Parables Summary Multiple Paths From Bad To Good 249
Grace, Talents, and Works 250
The Grace Debate 252

Preface

The origins of this book began at a multidisciplinary hospital meeting in which I was asked at the last minute to provide the meditational moment. Up until that time our writings had focused on only Original Testament material. Since we had wanted to explore additional meanings for the New Testament, we asked this group to simply pick their favorite parable. My intention was to explore that parable at the moment and to generate ideas and directions for our next book. We went half way around the room of this group of church going believers from diverse backgrounds before anyone could come up with a single answer. That choice was Jesus feeding the 5000 people.

I realized then that we had a huge task to refamiliarize modern readers with something that was only familiar at a cursory level. I challenged my co-author Richard Huizenga for each of us to come up with our five favorite or most influential parables. We had something in mind like "The Gospel in 5 Parables" much like "A History Of The World In 100 Objects "by Neil MacGregor. That is we would take each five parables that we felt represented the gospel and expand upon them. This is, by the way, a useful exercise that many of you will find enjoyable and illuminating.

Our original list had the story of the Prodigal which contains many essential messages of the gospel while at the same time recognizing free will and repentance along with many other overlooked themes. The Good Samaritan had always inspired us as young children to capture the key element of inclusivity of the gospel. Now the choices became more difficult and our lists began to diverge.

The parable of the Sower seemed essential as did the parable of the Talents. But what about the unforgiving servant, the rich man who stores up treasures, the unjust judge, and many others?

When it dawned on us that the story told by Jesus in Matthew chapter 25 about the sheep and goats was actually a parable, we had an epiphany. Our seemingly overly ambitious task of narrowing down the gospel to 5 stories could actually be reduced to 2 parables and still capture the essence. Furthermore these 2 parables capture the dual meanings we listed for offensive up front. The Prodigal is full of offense by first the younger son, then the elder, and other subtle offenses.

The story of the Prodigal captures the first definition of offensive with its insults while the story of the sheep and goats captures the definition involving challenge. The story of the sheep and goats seems real enough, yet is meant to provoke us into action here and now and not in some far off mythical land or futuristic setting. These 2 meanings of offensive can be captured somewhat by the word confrontational. In this sense we wish to confront you with our work by inspiring you to take a fresh look at the gospels which will hopefully motivate you into action. Obviously, symbols are a key part to appreciating the gospels. Humor, on the other hand has a surprising role.

Introduction

The Offensive Gospel

The Gospel will at times offend our sensibilities. In so doing there is an opportunity to startle us simultaneously into action. The offensive gospel allows us to break from the status quo and become more inclusive. Some of the offense of the gospel seems rather obvious at first glance but perhaps has a deeper meanings than we otherwise wish to recognize.

Take for example the Good Samaritan. Our initial reaction is to celebrate the fact that a foreigner does the humane act that the pious religious individuals do not. This seems like inclusion and indeed it is if that is as far as we go. What we are meant to do though is to examine the pious individuals who turned their back on an opportunity for assistance and then to ask ourselves how we do the same on a daily basis. Therefore the offense that we feel for the piety is directed inwardly at ourselves.

On a different level we might turn to the story of Mary and Martha. We are no doubt a little offended that Martha does not get credit for the work that she is doing. We assuage ourselves by noting that the master has decreed that listening to him is more important. Even so we are offended because the message is rather one sided.

Return next to the story of the unjust judge. Here our offense comes from the fact that the woman is persistent to the point of being obnoxious at the most inopportune time. This cuts to our own sensibilities and we are irritated even if we wish to celebrate her persistence.

Perhaps no where do you sense the offensiveness of the Gospels anymore then in the parable of the talents. In this parable people are not given the same amount of talents and there seems to be different expectations accordingly. The master returns with rather exacting demands.

Along the same lines is the story of the vineyard workers. The workers who work only the last hour are paid as much as those who worked all day. So too the thief on the cross seems to have a last-minute pardon despite a life of debauchery.

One of the time honored classics which causes us to have offense is the story of the prodigal son. In this situation the son squanders his inheritance only to return to the willing arms of his father. We displace our disgust for the prodigal because of the older brother's behavior, however to be sure we are offended because the older brother has indeed a very good point.

Sometimes there appears to be a set up to rile us up and lose sight perhaps of a personal message. One such story is of the man who is forgiven a large sum and then wishes to extract a very small sum from a petty servant. In each of these stories we believe we are meant to feel the finger pointing back at us much like it did with the prophet Naaman when he confronted King David.

Along the lines of forgiveness we are reminded that if we are offering our gift at the altar, we are to go and make it right with our brother before we can offer our gift. The implication here is that it does not matter who is right or wrong. And when we are right that is very offensive.

Sometimes we are so offended that we are not sure if we should be offended at Jesus or the disciples when in reality there's perhaps another choice. The woman who touched Jesus cloak is a classic example of this type. Either Jesus or the disciples seem a bit too sensitive about the whole process or better yet insensitive. There is no doubt a message there for us if we are willing to examine our own inner being.

Sometimes these stories or parables seem so obvious that they are not for us. For example there is the story of the rich man who says to himself that he is going to tear down his barns and build bigger ones and then sit back and eat drink and be merry. Surely Jesus meant this as a warning to anybody who thought they had acquired enough wealth or possessions on their own. What if the real message for this story was that the man's soul was required of him that day because he actually stopped growing? When someone reads through any version of the story it is certainly plausible that this is the meaning and we miss the offense that we are all supposed to feel because we are all supposed to keep growing much again like the parable of the talents.

In summary it may be helpful to take a second look at the stories and parables of the Gospel. If we do so and remove our own prejudice and try to place ourselves in the center of the story and be honest about how we ourselves are the individual involved, then we may have occasion to invoke a true change and be more inclusive and representative of God's love to all of God's children.

The Hopefully Inoffensive Gospel

We had pretty much finished our book on parables when we came across the work Short Stories by Jesus author Amy Jill Levine. Her insights are worth reading to have a healthy lens. We would certainly agree that the parables are all told for multiple meanings and that those who see only one meaning are generally limited, biased, and possibly prejudiced. That prejudice may have significant anti-Semitic tones that we hope we are not guilty of.

While Levine reminds us of the humor that was intended behind many of the parables, we may have simultaneously that nervous laughter that there is a deeper implied social challenge that we are not fully comfortable with. They are, as she notes, invitations without having to have an answer. They were not told so much as to be meaningful as to be perpetual meaning making devices. They are playful devices that are not to be toyed with even as we reflect again and again.

The distinction that Levine makes between parables and allegories is a useful distinction. She is emphatic that these stories are not allegorical. Nor are they autobiographical. Nor are they meant to be mere platitudes or even stories of assurance. The characters of the stories are on the one hand familiar and yet paradoxically there is at the same time a sense of strangeness that we are not quite comfortable with.

Indeed there is a play on stereotypes that is meant to challenge our own stereotypes. Ironically the traditional Christian lens often looks at many of the parables as pointing a strong finger at the Jewish leaders of Jesus time. What if many such individuals were as engaged in these stories as you and I can be. What if they sensed the playful, humorous yet challenging opportunity to re-examine our actions?

Indeed the parables were told not so much to be social commentary as to be socially challenging and provocative. To see any parable as not having a fresh message for us today is to limit the power of parables to inspire that social change. To limit the parables to one interpretation is to limit ourselves, but not the parables themselves. To see the parables as judgement to a group Jesus was opposed to is to both miss his connection with them, and the challenges for ourselves.

When it is all said and done we still feel that the Parable of the Prodigal along with the Sheep and Goats parable are most representative of the gospel. They challenge our stereotypes of situations if we allow ourselves to at the same time realize some of the context that they were told while also realizing their application for our times. Each parable has its own social challenge. Neither is truly judgmental but each recalls in the words of Emerson that a wise person judges no one. He simply lets people judge themselves and merely records the verdict.

Symbols

The parables frequently deal with a variety of people and situations drawn from Jewish culture of Jesus' time. Most people are identified by their role in the culture, sometimes named by label or station and sometimes simple as an unnamed "person". The question being should we limit our understanding of the situation to the Biblical description or should we, or could we, enlarge our understanding by thinking of the situation or person as a symbol?

For example, the parables usually name a person by role or title such as a Pharisee or Ruler or Tax Collector. As such they are a symbol of that role and frequently that carries with it another symbol, a preconceived view of how that person thinks or conducts them self. Many times the parable uses that preconception to illustrate or reach a conclusion, such as in the Good Samaritan when the Pharisee turns up his nose at the injured traveler-he's on more important business than helping a person below his station. In the same parable, the Samaritan, a societal outcast, does take the time and effort to help and rescue the man beset, beaten and robbed by thieves The Pharisee, a symbol of arrogance and power, satisfies one symbol, power; but does nothing to satisfy another symbol of his role, to render help when it's needed. Instead he satisfies the symbol of arrogance. The Samaritan surprises us. Instead of showing himself a lowlife outcast, he becomes our hero, demonstrating empathy, rescue, healing and generosity, none of which you expect from a social outcast.

In the same way, you find parable character symbols that take you to a normal or expected place, but their actions could take you to another place. And in that other symbolic place, you find the real meaning of the parable.

Consider the Prodigal son symbols. The father, the prodigal son, the feast, the good son At the surface, it's a good moral story A kind father has a younger son that wants to flex his wings, ask the father for an early inheritance and goes off and has a good time in the city. But, alas, he squanders his time and money, falls on hard times and decides to go back and beg forgiveness. It worked. The father welcomes him with a meal, a bath and new clothes. Father hopes his son learned his lesson and son is back in the family. Lesson: A good father gives his kid a second chance at home if they stray and repent, even though his other kids are and remain upset with the foolish son. The good kids should just "get over it".

That's one set of symbols. Another set could be deeper, having to do with our modern culture and with a father who is God, a prodigal son who is a typical youngster trying to loosen restraints on for an exciting lifestyle and a good older and focused son who is happy with some lifestyle constraints. Play the same flexing of the younger son's scenario out and you could be looking at a sinner confessing his mistakes to God, who forgives, returns him to his favor and the benefits of righteousness. The older son sadly, earns no additional favor for his faithful righteousness, but is still invited to continue the favor of righteousness. It's an even handed symbol of justice; you all get the same reward if you affirm the covenant.

In fact you can find multiple symbols in all the Parables. The obvious level that Jesus was trying to get his followers to see and understand the meanings and symbols consistent with the popular labels for the characters and their actions in the contemporary culture. There is also at least one deeper level for every parable. That level is unique for every listener who understands and processes the parables meaning as it's heard; it's the level where the symbolic meaning is applied to heart and then generates a changed life or at least changed behavior.

Humor

Humor can occur at a number of different levels, such as by the traditional "at the expense of others", or by unequal comparisons, or using words out of context. Humor can also occur when a negative situation ends with a positive experience; it doesn't have to produce a laugh. Normally, we would not think of humor as an emotion present in the Bible or the serious teachings and lessons within the parables. After all, the parables are serious stuff, life lessons that we are take to heart, not funny, not to be dismissed as a momentary pleasure. Humor is part of the leavening experience, allowing us to absorb the facts of our situation, to put it into perspective, to see ourselves in the story if we allow that to happen. So, the fact is, that humor can be of necessity present in the parables and other biblical human experience stories. Sometimes hidden, but there nonetheless.

The wedding feast at Cana is one example where Jesus' mother Mary comes to him with a problem - "They're out of Wine". He seems slightly offended, thinking probably "what do you want me to do about it"? Then, after convincing Jesus he should do something about the "it", Mary goes to the hired help that are filling the water jars and tells them to pay attention to Jesus' requests- Mom showing her intervention tendencies, probably prompting some jokes, even by Jesus, at her expense.

At some level, humor is everywhere in Jesus' parables. Maybe not always in the direct players, but in and by the imagined onlookers within the thumbnail plays -the onlookers seeing the participants, making their mistakes, laughing, shaking their heads in anticipation of the consequences, clicking their tongues at their foolishness, or laughing again when they get put out in the cold like the Foolish Virgins. Jesus' audiences would have listened and in their mind's eye seen the consequences of the players in the stories, even the hero, anti hero, and the victim in the Good Samaritan.

Read the Parables, always looking for the humor as well as the intended meaning or Dogma of each parable. Then compare the characters to contemporary culture.

Between 2 Parables.

When we reflected further we recognized that argument can be made that the majority of the parables and even the majority of the gospels can be summarized by 2 parables. The first is the story of the prodigal which occurs in the heart of the gospel of Luke in chapter 15. The second occurs at the latter part of Matthew in chapter 25. It is paradoxically easy for us to write ourselves into both of these parables as well as to write ourselves out of them. These parables seem somehow meant for us while at the same time, not quite. We would never be as judgmental as the elder brother even though we would like to believe that Jesus is waiting for us on our return. We would like to believe that we are not like the goats who either did not recognize Jesus or did not attend to him in his hour of need.

Once we remove the sentimentality that surrounds our own moment of prodigal return, we have to wrestle with our other roles as the older brother. We are comfortable with that elder brother representing the religious leaders that were present for the listening, but in no way can we see this as meant for our own blinders. We may all too easily dismiss any chance of playing the role of the father because that makes us compare ourselves to God the Father. That also may require us to be more tolerant of differences than we might care to be. It might require us to confront the older rigid way of thinking that we would rather not, because we too are ensconced in it. Meanwhile we would rather wallow in the sentimentality, much as the prodigal would have gladly mixed in with the pigs for his own sustenance.

For our back cover of the book on parables we choose the parable of the sheep and goats in Matthew chapter 25. This is sometimes overlooked as a parable by those who enumerate them, though it certainly fulfills all the criteria for parables. The problem is that it is a picture story with imagery that is all too real. How can we possibly know the many disguises of Jesus. We wish to find ourselves among the sheep at the end of the day, at the end of the story, at the end of life, at the brink of eternity. But we would feel a little more comfortable if there was some means testing or at least some way to recognize the many disguises Jesus represents.

Identity

CHAPTER 1

Humble Birth

We celebrate the birth of a little child in the most humble circumstances on a regular basis. That baby, after all, represents so much of what we would like to believe. We would like to think that any of us can have rather humble origins and still accomplish great things on this earth. By providing the lineage or ancestry of Jesus we establish an ongoing line since the recorded history. We establish that there is a royal background that is shared. That royal background also connects the baby with a religious background that is by design connected to the perpetuity of that royal line.

Jesus Birth to the Disciples

When we look at the gospel it may help to try to experience it from the original perspective. If we do so we may see the potential offensiveness from the beginning. During the conception we see that we have a young unwed mother who is pregnant. In hindsight we soothe ourselves by saying this is an immaculate conception by God and then we can move on.

Nonetheless, we must feel that the first generation still felt the sting of potential scandal and left echoes of such in the gospels. Alternatively, we might look at works like "Born of a Woman" by John Shelby Spong where he presents his case that the bigger offense is where we insert God into the conception role instead of allowing what he could make of one of the ultimate outcasts of the time. We would be further troubled that God could not use the conventional religious traditions of the time to introduce the Messiah. We would add to the offense by noting that he approved of foreign dignitaries lying to the local political structure when the wise man avoided their pledge to tell Herod about the Christ child.

Next we would question the nature of a child who had the audacity to sit with revered religious leaders at the tender age of 12, while his parents looked frantically for him.

We can sweep all this under the carpet until we get to the first miracle where Jesus turns the water to wine at the wedding. Here we have Jesus seeming to talk down to his own mother Mary about why she is bothering him. Let's add to the challenge of potential offense and site from the same book above by noting John Shelby Spong. He notes that why else would Mary be bothering Jesus at the wedding, unless she was the mother of the groom. Our purpose here though is to not remove ourselves to too much unprovable, but to simply look at what's there in a potentially new light.

Let's move on in the life of Jesus ever trying to keep in mind the first generation of exposure. Jesus is going to call a number of relatively low life to be his disciples. Some of these will be married men like Peter who will be asked to leave behind their families while they pursue an agenda that may be antagonist to the religious and government authorities. Is it any wonder that towards the end of Jesus career that someone like Peter would interpret his duty to take a sword and cut off a soldier's ear after that soldier had been sent by the religious authorities to arrest Jesus? We have to acknowledge that we would be offended if we were in that first generation.

Matthew Advent

When we reflect on advent we realize that there are many ways for the light of the world to be born. The gospels basically present four separate and yet related at some rudimentary level version of how the light of the world may enter. We must look at all of these versions to have the most complete picture for the world. Yet the individual may identify with one of the particular versions and that is the beauty of Advent.

Most of the time we identify with the Christmas story with some blend of at least the first three Gospels Matthew, Mark, and Luke. The reality is that they are very separate stories although there are a few common features. Only the gospel of Matthew has the story of the Wise men. Only in the Gospel of Luke do the angels speak to Mary. And despite being a synoptic gospel, Mark does not mention the birth of Jesus whatsoever.

The Gospel of Matthew begins with a very patriarchal approach by giving a long lineage that culminates in the birth of Jesus. Accordingly it mentions only males in the long genealogy. It also begins with Abraham who was of course the father of the whole Jewish line. Since it is male oriented there is a point of the 14 generations from Abraham to David and 14 generations from David to the exile and 14 generations from the exile to the birth of Christ. This is a classic male fixation on numbers.

With its male orientation the angel of the Lord will appear to Joseph in a dream but there will be no visit of angel to Mary as occurs in the Gospel of Luke. The dream connection is to solidify the connection with the original Old Testament Joseph who was the great grandson of Abraham and himself was a man noted for his dreams. The male emphasis will continue with the foreign magi who have a vision that an important leader has been born.

The magi are men only. Being men they were allowed to have their own dream with a warning not to return the same way they came in therefore avoid King Herod who had evil designs for the baby Jesus. This will be followed by another dream from an angel to Joseph to take the child and flee to a foreign country in order to do the male role of protection. Then following the death of Herod the angel of the Lord will appear once more to Joseph in a dream telling him it is safe to return with the family to Israel.

Mark Advent

The fundamental Gospel of Mark wishes to dispense of any protracted human linage for Jesus Christ. Rather in chapter 1 verse one we see that Jesus is described right off the bat as the son of God. Yes the message of the gospel of Mark is a different type of birth. Even the forerunner of Jesus, namely John the Baptist, will talk about being born again with the baptism of the Holy Spirit.

Following Jesus baptism he will call his own disciples and as he tells them he will show them how to be fishers of men. The first act that he does out of deliberation will be to drive out an impure spirit. Essentially this is a new birth for this man as well. The word of Jesus is recognized as both a new teaching and simultaneously with authority by this act of rebirth for the impure.

When we turn to the gospel of Luke we see a different approach with some common themes. First an angel of the Lord will appear to a male named Zachariah who will not believe that his wife is going to conceive in her old age. Therefore it was time for the women to get involved and the angel Gabriel appeared to Mary and gave her the news of the forthcoming birth of the Savior through her. Mary is allowed to ask questions without impunity unlike Zachariah.

The theme of the importance of women will continue as Mary meets up with her cousin Elizabeth who will be the mother of John the Baptist. Once again the Holy Spirit is involved in this interaction. Eventually the humble shepherds will be told of the immaculate birth of Jesus through an angel of the Lord as well. After the dedication the story of Jesus and the baptism of Jesus we have the genealogy of Jesus extending all the way back to God. The difference between he and Matthew is that Luke gives the actual people between Jesus and God. In addition we have the mention of four women and the lineage of Jesus as though God had the female connection and importance in mind all along.

John Advent

We next turn to the mystical gospel of John and see a whole other dimension of the concept of the birth of Jesus. There he is described as the Word as well as the light of all mankind. The Word always was and did not need to be birthed but did choose to become flesh and live among humans. The "Word" in fact was present at creation as God "Spoke" all things into creation. The gospel of John gives birth to mystery and paradox. John the Baptist summarizes this aptly in his introduction to Jesus saying that a man who comes after me has surpassed me because he was before me.

In summary the Gospels collectively give us a choice of how we wish to see the birth of the Savior into our world. We may look at that birth through a patriarchal lens as in Matthew or through a matriarchal lens as in Luke. We can minimize the human dimension in the Gospel of Mark and virtually eliminated altogether in the gospel of John. The genius of these wide ranging choices of birth is literally difficult to conceive.

Stephen Harrison and Richard Huizinga

Luke Humor and Advent Part 1

Imagine a sitcom in which a male figure is given a certain amount of information and then asks a question for verification only to be struck deaf for a sign of what is to come. Then later in the same episode we have a young female given a fair amount of important information who asks a similar type of question. In the female situation though there is a blessing which is bestowed upon her and the promise that her child will have great prominence. We would have to see the humor even today.

That is of course what happens in the first chapter of the Gospel of Luke. The uncle of Jesus namely Zechariah is visited by an angel and told that his wife will have a son who will be a forerunner prophet to prepare the way for the Lord. Zechariah responds by asking how he can be sure of this. It does not seem like an unreasonable request since his wife is rather old. The angel making the presentation though senses that it is not merely a conjecture but rather a question of disbelief.

Next return to the story of Mary's visit by the angel. In this situation Mary is also given news that she has found favor with God and will give birth to a son who ultimately will be called the son of God. Mary also has the audacity to ask the question of how this could be since she was a virgin. Arguably this is a reasonable question though one that is more readily solvable by her simply getting married and having a partner supply the seed. In other words she was not instructed to remain a virgin.

To be sure we are told that Mary was a virgin at the time but also engaged to a man named Joseph. That engagement is reaffirmed when we come to chapter 2 of Luke and we are told that Joseph needs to go and register for the taxation. Because they are of the house of David they journey to Bethlehem where Mary delivers a baby and has to lay him in a Manger because of the lack of space available. This is followed by the traditional shepherd pageantry after the angel versus the shepherds.

Parables and Paradox

The shepherds of course are visited by an angel who is identified as the angel of the Lord. We don't really know if this is the same angel that appeared in any of the first two angel encounters. What we do know is that angels and their appearance has a habit of startling people or making them afraid or even terrifying them depending on which encounter we are discussing. In fact that progression of fear is the exact level of description applied in the Gospel of Luke.

Either God or the angels might have had some sense of humor because they learned from their experience of encounters. In the first encounter Zechariah was told not to be afraid but certainly was. Mary was told not to be afraid but certainly was. The shepherds likewise were told not to be afraid even though they were terrified. But angels are also on the learning curve here. In the first encounter they gave a sign that no one would want. In the second encounter they give a sign that anyone would be happy with. In the third encounter they volunteer a sign without being asked. Humor amidst fear.

Humor in Luke's Advent Part 2

The early chapters of the Gospel of Luke and in particular the advent story is that of contrast and dichotomy. One of the biggest contrasts occurs in the male and female dichotomy. The gospel begins with an introduction to a male by a male. Then to make sure that we have the significance of the time we will be told that the next key player is a man by the name of Zechariah who lived in the time of King Herod. In Luke we do not get the destructive testosterone side of the king that we do in Matthew, but that is an external contrast.

Zechatiah is performing a duty in the temple that only a male can do. This is despite the subtle notion we are given that both he and his wife are both righteous. We are given the impression that he was on duty by chance, perhaps implying that God can either use elements of chance, or whoever happens to be around. Surely God did not employ the appearance of chance when his hand was all the time behind this? Either way the man who is chosen for a very holy duty is about to be scared voiceless by an angel of God. The angel was of course, male. Indeed, no named angels in the Bible are women.

Just as Herod has been silenced by Luke, so too will Zechariah be silenced by an angel when he does question the angel, seemingly in disbelief. We have noted elsewhere the difference in outcome when the male Zechariah questions an angel as contrasted with the female Mary who is also startled by an angel. In her situation though the female is rewarded for her questions. Doesn't seem quite fair unless we recognize that God and angels look at attitude or are establishing a new approach. Or both.

We are going to have the introduction of a new way of thinking come to us by way of a teenage girl who is pregnant and not married. There will be some potential scandal over this that is more hinted about in the gospel of Matthew where Joseph contemplates divorce because of this. Following Mary's angel encounter her cousin Elizabeth and the baby in her cousin's womb will recognize the significance of what Mary represents. Mary responds with her longest and most famous speech.

What is notable in Luke is that we are told at the start of her great speech that it is her own soul and her own spirit that recognizes great truths and contrasts. She recounts the endless mercy of God and simultaneously the endless recognition of her role forever by humanity. She contrasts the prior success of the proud, and rulers, and rich (think men) with those who are humble and hungry (disproportionately women). They are hungry for something new yet at the same time connected with the rich past of Abraham.

We are not done with the male aspect quite yet. Seemingly we will have some restoration of such when Zechariah gets his voice back. His speech is, after all, longer than Mary's. More notably, it is inspired by the universal Holy Spirit, and not his own, unlike Mary. The first half recalls traditional male themes of protection from enemies and a connection with "father" Abraham. The second half recognizes more universal gender neutral themes of salvation, forgiveness, mercy, and a light for all living in darkness.

The male and female elements will blend together as the baby Jesus is dedicated at the temple. Both male and female sources recognize the significance of Jesus. Once again, though, such recognition seems to come to the female naturally whereas the male requires inspiration from the Holy Spirit. Both parents follow the traditions of their religion in a supportive fashion. The child is inspired to go to the traditional male leaders and amaze them with new ways of thinking.

Seemingly we return to male vestiges when we have the long linage of Jesus with males only, unlike the gospel of Matthew which mentions a series of females. Luke's long linage ends with Adam who is called the son of God in chapter 3. Satan is the only other figure who capitalizes on this term son of God when he tempts Jesus with that very title in the next chapter. While we see Jesus deflect the earthly temptation we are left wondering if this was a subtle yet humorous way of God putting to rest the traditional male significance and its misapplication of power.

I am statements in John part 1

To find out how Jesus defines himself, we turn to the gospel, John, to use his own words of who he is. There is a popular site on the internet that gives some nice metaphors for statements in John by Jesus referenced as the *seven I Am statements*. As useful as those real metaphors are for some tidy theology, the reality is that there are a lot more statements that Jesus uses as self descriptive in the book of John. The Gospel of John might even be called the I Am book. We reference elsewhere how Jesus refers to himself as the Messiah to the woman at the well in the fourth chapter of John. This is in the form of an "I Am" statement referencing that he is the Messiah when "I Am he" is used. The Messiah however is not a king who sits back and is waited upon. Rather he is as the next chapter of John reveals in the fifth chapter verse 36 that I am doing the work of God. In other words *I am* one who does the work of God.

The next reference is not a direct statement but as a strong self descriptor it shares that equivalent impact. The setting is in the sixth chapter of John in which Jesus has been witnessed by the disciples to be walking on the water. As Jesus approaches the boat they are in they are indeed terrified. Jesus responds to them to not be afraid because I*t is I*. The meaning behind this simple phrase is extensive. Certainly it implies that Jesus is still himself even after he appears to be doing something highly irregular. He is also one who is a comforter as he attempts to assuage their fear. He is not a supernatural or apparition to fear.

Later in the sixth chapter of John we receive the image of the bread of life when Jesus says *I am the bread of life*. This is the first of the traditional seven metaphors made with *I Am* statements. The others later in the chapter include *I am* the light of the world in John chapter 8, *I am* the gate in John chapter 10, *I am* the good shepherd and John chapter 10, *I am* the resurrection and the life in chapter 11, *I am* the way truth and the life, in John in chapter 14 and finally *I am* the true vine found in John chapter 15.

The final equivalent of an *I am* statement in the sixth chapter of John is found in verse 63 in which Jesus says the words, *I have spoken to you are spirit and they are life*. Even his words have existential meaning.

This is reminiscent of the first chapter of John where the word became flesh and dwelt among us.

The seventh chapter of John has an unusual position for an I am statement by Jesus. There he is talking to the Jewish leaders and tells them unexpectedly that, *Yes you know me and you know where I am from and that I am not here on my own* in verse 28.

We are not accustomed to Jesus acknowledging that the Jewish leaders know him. Later in the chapter in verse 33 Jesus tells the disciples that, *I am with you for only a short time* before he goes to God. In the very next verse Jesus says, *where I am you cannot come.*

In John chapter 8 we see in verse 16 that Jesus says, *I am not alone but stand with the Father who sent me*. In verse 18 he says that *I am one who testifies for myself* then acknowledges that his other witness is the Father who sent him. Later in verse 21 he states that *I am going away* and that where he goes we cannot come. In verse 28 Jesus knows that *I am* the one I claim to be. In verse 38 Jesus says, *I am telling you what I have seen in the Father's presence.* In other words, I am one who reveals important hidden truths. Later in the chapter in verse 49 Jesus will say that I am not possessed by a demon. In the following verse he will say that *I am not seeking glory for myself.* To close off this great chapter of I Am statements Jesus references the patriarch Abraham and makes the statement before Abraham was born, *I am.* This of course was the classic statement made by God in the Old Testament. It needs no further definition and indeed cannot be followed by an adequate description.

Redemption Circle – The Not So Missing Link

The Circle of Righteousness is based on these references in Scripture, all point to faith as the basis of being judged or counted Righteous, either by a direct statement or by implication. They are: Genesis 15:6, Romans

4:3 & 22, and John 8:56 & 58. In Genesis God directly credits Abraham's belief as Righteousness and Paul twice confirms that directly in Romans. In John, Jesus debates his divinity with the Pharisees and places himself first at Creation, then with the Father and Abraham, implying that he was there as a witness and participant.

These verses in John, coupled with the others, resemble a Redemption circle from creation's past, to Abraham's antiquity, to the Cross, to our present, to the unknown future. Or maybe, Redemption has always been present, part of a plan.

The statement in Genesis that Abraham believed in God and his belief was "counted as Righteousness" comes as a shock because his belief is not linked to Christ's far in the future death on the cross as the basis of salvation and righteousness. However, Romans 4 makes it clear that Abraham's belief in God, (the Triune God as we know it now) was the basis for his imputed righteousness. A belief in Christ today or a sincere belief by Original Testament Believers is the same basis for imputed righteousness. In the Original Testament, the atonement sacrifice looked forward to Christ's death on the cross, the enabler for all ages that, through faith, transfers, imputes, His righteousness to the believer.

Isaiah captures that future event with the prophecy "the punishment due us was upon him." Luther coined the term for this justified state: "at the same time, sinner and justified".

The fact that Abraham lived in the Original Testament and Christ's death occurred in the New Testament does not negate the nature of faith or belief for all believers. The same triune God was present for all time periods on earth and none of his acts or judgments are limited by time. One act, the cross, enables the imputation of righteousness retroactively to Original Testament believers and concurrently to New Testament believers as they come to faith in Christ.

I Am statements – As Metaphors

We move from the existential *I Am* statement where basically Jesus uses the identity of the indescribable God by giving another metaphor so that we humans can at least have some appreciation of an image that we ourselves may identify with. In John 9:5 we hear Jesus saying that *I am the light of the world*. We would do well to recall that the preface to this statement is that *while I am in this world*. Perhaps we are meant to pair this with statements made elsewhere in the Sermon on the Mount where Jesus says to those believers listening that they are the light of the world. This statement comes in the context of healing a man born blind. We are meant to appreciate the deeper metaphor that the religious leader's blindness is analogous to the physical blindness. This may occur when we insert our own *I Am* statements of ourselves or use the symbols and metaphors of God for God himself.

The next *I Am* statements will occur in chapter 10 where Jesus first says that he is the gate for the sheep and then later that he is the good shepherd. He notes that such a shepherd will sacrifice all for the sheep. The good news here is that such includes any single dumb sheep that has been led astray. In this analogy the good shepherd is one who is the owner and also knows all the sheep. Furthermore the sheep know the owner just as Jesus knows God the Father, as the analogy continues. We sometimes conveniently ignore the part that follows where Jesus says that he has sheep from another fold. This is meant to be an inclusive statement that we may be blinded just like the religious leaders referred to in chapter 9. Finally before closing this sheep analogy, Jesus makes a direct statement for those that may have missed the meaning of the sheep metaphor: I and the Father are one. United. Inclusive.

Next we have in John chapter 11 the resurrection of Lazarus. Here we have the recognition of Martha that Jesus is the Christ as we have detailed elsewhere. Jesus says, first to her that *I am the resurrection and the life. He that believes in me will live, even though he dies.* Jesus symbolizes all that has been dead but can be called back to life including faith and even dead symbols for God. Those symbols include all symbols that pretend to be more than the original I Am or separate from the I Am or dead in any other way. Jesus notes this concept in John chapter 12 where he states that unless a grain of wheat falls to the ground and dies, it bears no fruit. There follows another comparison about eternal life for he who hates his life in the world. Yes, of course this in an analogy. We are not literally meant to hate our world. But if we get lost with trying to overuse the death of Christ on the cross in unintended ways, then we may miss the final *I Am* statement of chapter 12 verse 26. There Jesus states that where *I am*, my servant also will be. We are indeed meant to serve.

John and Metaphors part 1

When a master poet by the name of Robert Frost wrote an essay about being at home with the metaphor, he was not introducing a new concept or genre. By the same token the author of the gospel of John did not introduce the concept of metaphor but took it to a higher level. We would do well to consider some of those metaphors and their implications for our life today. Keep in mind that a metaphor like any symbol is representative of a truth above and beyond itself.

In this essay we will examine the seven "I Am" statements that are metaphorical from the words of Jesus himself. We will examine additional metaphors keeping in mind that the gospel of John opens with a strong suit of metaphor. In the first sentence we see that Jesus was identified as the Word who is with God from the beginning and also actually was God and by implication still is. These are existential statements that mostly dwell in the past tense.

We believe that we are meant to see that the historical events are indeed history and in a sense living but that they live through the metaphor. Accordingly we see in verse one in the beginning was the Word. Next we have the Word was with God. Next we have the Word was God. Finally we have he was with God in the beginning. The human mind will naturally ask themselves how something can be both God and with God at the same time.

It is of course a living metaphor that allows this to happen. We are not even given the earthly name of Jesus until verse 17 of the first chapter. Before that we are given the name of his forerunner John the Baptist of whom it was said was not himself the light. One of the rare uses of the present tense In chapter 1 comes in verse 15 where we see that the statement John testifies as in the present as opposed to the past tense used exclusively until that point.

John the Baptist begins his definition along with the author of the gospel as first what he is not. In verse eight we read that he was not the light. In verse 20 we have his first statement in the present I am not the Christ. Then he tells them he is not Elijah or the prophet. His first self definition in the present is I am the voice of one calling in the desert to make straight the way for the Lord. Even in using this I am statement he is quoting from the past through the prophet Isaiah.

It is no less than John the Baptist who uses the first present tense living metaphor to describe Jesus. In verse 20 he told those present to behold the Lamb of God who takes away the sin of the world. The next day he repeats the same metaphor to describe Jesus. John the Baptist also describes the fact that he baptizes people symbolically with water but that Jesus will baptize people with the Holy Spirit. Both John and Jesus will baptize us with rich metaphors.

Stephen Harrison and Richard Huizinga

John Metaphors part 2

Now that we have the description of John the Baptist and metaphors that have been attributed to Jesus, it is time to examine the I Am metaphors that Jesus himself employs. The first I Am metaphor occurs in John chapter 6 verse 35 in which Jesus says I am the bread of life. The context follows his feeding of 5000 people actual physical bread. The followers understand the connection between that power and a belief system and ask Jesus following the event to explain the connection.

The crowd understandably seeks a sign in the form of a miracle. They reference Moses giving them bread from heaven but Jesus points out that that actually came from God the father. Furthermore he points out that the bread of God is he who comes down from heaven and gives life to the world. When the crowd asks for that bread Jesus points out clearly the first I am statement by noting that he is the bread of life having come down from heaven.

The next I Am statement of Jesus comes in John chapter 8 verse 12 in which he says I am the light of the world. Once again the context is very important. We have preceding this statement the apocryphal inclusion involving the woman caught in the act of adultery who is brought to Jesus to assist with her condemnation. Jesus resists the setup by the religious leaders to condemn her and rather asks that each of them examine their own conscience.

The phrasing of verse 12 seems to add credence to the actual offense in the first 11 verses. In verse 12 we see the statement when Jesus spoke again to the people which implies a distinction of dealing with the religious leaders in the preceding event. He tells the people that whoever follows him will not walk in darkness (as the woman caught in adultery had done) but would rather have the light of life. After a heated exchange with the religious leaders and reference to father Abraham, Jesus uses the statement that before Abraham was born, I am. This existential I Am statement equates himself with God.

The next metaphor is actually a paired metaphor which occurs in the 10th chapter of John. In verse seven we read that I am the gate for the sheep. A few verses later we read I am the good shepherd. Of course both of these are related metaphors and are paired on purpose. We are even told in verse six of the 10th chapter of John that Jesus used a figure of speech but that they did not understand what he was telling them.

The context of this metaphor occurs after Jesus has healed someone who is was physically blind. Ironically he is pointing out to the religious leaders that they are the ones that are blind metaphorically speaking. By the same token we maintain that those who take the words of Jesus solely on their literal basis without the symbolic meaning also do not understand Jesus or his meaning for us today.

John Metaphors part 3

Jesus makes and I Am statement in John chapter 11 that some scholars count as a metaphor. In verse 25 he says I am the resurrection and the life. Is it includes the paradox that the one who believes in Jesus will live even though they die and then in the next verse notes that whoever lives by believing in him will never die. While this group of statements is convoluted and paradoxical the immediate response for the intended party of Martha is that she indeed does believe that process.

Of course she would very much like for her dead brother Lazarus to rise again and Martha makes the bold statement that she knows he will rise again in the resurrection at the last day. That is when Jesus makes his most interesting statement that he is both the resurrection and the life. Now to be clear at this point he has not been sacrificed and therefore we must factor that very important element. This leaves us little choice but to treat his words that he is the resurrection as symbolic.

It may be rather fitting that this resurrection statement is part of the convenient formula for the life of a Christian except that it does not march out in this context. Rather we believe that this is another I am statement meant as a metaphor in which Jesus is bringing to life all that is dead in traditional religion. He is at the same time alive in the now. He may therefore talk symbolically about physical death in the same breath that he talks about never dying spiritually.

A few chapters later in John chapter 14 Jesus will tell the troubled disciples that he is the way and the truth and the life. This is once again done in the form of and I Am statement. This is followed by the statement that no one comes to the father except through me which certainly has to include the concept that no one comes to the father except by the truth. In the next chapter we see the evidence of love for Jesus which is obeying his commandments as in loving one another.

This brings us to the final I am a metaphor in the gospel of John found in chapter 15. Their Jesus says that I am the true vine and my father is the gardener. Besides cutting off branches that don't bear fruit he also prunes the branches that do bear fruit in order that they may vary even more. When something is pruned it is often necessary to remove the dead elements that are inhibiting further growth. Once again we therefore see the meaning of a living resurrection in which the dead is restored to life.

In summary the seven I Am metaphors found in the gospel of John reveal profound truths and deep paradoxes. They symbolize getting our daily bread as well as lighting up the world. They are at the same time both the gate and the gate keeper for the sheep. They are simultaneously the resurrection and the life. They are perpetually the way and the life by displaying the truth. Sometimes the truth must grow paradoxically by cutting off the dead symbols of the unresurrected past to display light and life.

I Am Statements – The Future Revealed

We will see the intersection of the concept of servant along with the medical field in the next I Am statement found in John 13:13. There we see Jesus say that you call me teacher, for so I am. He goes on to point out that as the teacher, he leads by example including the humble example of washing feet. When we examine the root meaning of the word doctor, we find that it means to teach. Every doctor has had the experience of doing the grunge work somewhere along the line, and the best are still willing to do it again even when less skilled personnel are there to perform the perfunctory measures. Later in chapter 13 we have an *I Am* statement that notes that Jesus is one who reveals measures, and at the right time. In verse 19 we read "I am telling you now before it happens, so that when it does happen, you will believe that *I am* He." (NIV)

Towards the end of chapter 13 we begin a series of statements that the disciples have a hard time following in the moment. In verse 36 Jesus says that where I am going, you cannot follow now, but you will follow later. Then in chapter 14 we learn in Jesus words that "I am going to prepare a place for you." Then the chapter delivers strong I am statements about Jesus relationship with God. In verse 11 "*I am* in the Father and the Father in me". In verse 12 his statement that "I am going to the Father "leads to the possibility of us disciples doing greater works than we have seen in Jesus. That concept is strengthened further in verse 20: "....You will realize that I am in my Father, and you are in me, and I am in you. What we don't have there is the direct connection with ourselves to God, implying the need for intercessory.

We have a brief interlude in chapter 15 with the final picturesque metaphor of Jesus as the true vine. Here the message seems multifaceted in that we must bear fruit by branching out to be more inclusive. Then in chapter 16 we return to the notion of departure where Jesus says in verses 5,6 "I am going away for your own good." Paradoxically Jesus leaves us alone to bring us more comfort.

This leaves the resurrection where Jesus says to Mary to go tell others that "I am returning to my Father and to your Father, to my God and your God." The strongest connection we have with God is given to a woman after the resurrection in John 20:17. The final message of I am by Jesus comes in John 20:21 where Jesus says "Peace be with you! As the Father has sent me, *I am* sending you". (NIV) The use of the past tense has sent implies that the mission for Jesus is complete. We are to pick up the commission but the fulfillment of Jesus mission is given by him breathing on the disciples in order for them to have the Holy Spirit. What a picture painted in that last *I Am* encounter where Jesus gives peace while demonstrating his willingness to endure human suffering and at the same time giving us the one power that rivals the love of his sacrifice: forgiveness.

Recognizing the Messiah

Peter is often recognized as being the one who makes the great profession that Jesus is the Christ. In the 3 synoptic gospels, the setup is that Jesus first asks the disciples who people say Jesus is. Then Jesus asks them who do they say he is whereupon Peter professes that he is the Christ. But who is the first person to identify Jesus as the Christ? Who is the first adult? Who is the first who fully understands the meaning as the Christ? Who is the first to identify Jesus as the Christ without prompting? Does Jesus reveal himself as the Christ and people still don't recognize it?

Do some figure it out while we moderns don't? These thought provoking questions are meant to paint a composite picture of Jesus as the Christ that may shed some light for us moderns on the Light of the world.

For our purposes here we will generally confine our discussion to references that mention the Christ, or the Messiah, or God himself, or names that God uses for himself. We will exclude terms like the Son of Man, and even the Lamb of God, which are both terms certainly used by either Jesus or others to describe him that we very much recognize today as very important terminology for Jesus who was and is the Messiah Christ. Our rationale here is that such terms were not paired with Jesus and acknowledged by others as such. Therefore for our purposes here we exclude that statement made twice by John the Baptist about Jesus being the Lamb of God as Jesus does not use that term, no matter how important it may have been. Nor is it paired with the terminology of Christ, Messiah, or God. Likewise no one uses the term Son of Man as the Messiah in the New Testament, except for Christ himself.

Now what do we do with terms like the Son of God. That's certainly a pretty strong connection to God and certainly a term that we feel strongly about since God himself uses it in the gospel of John after the baptism by John of Jesus. If we allow this, then we may need to consider the revelation to Mary the mother of Jesus. In Luke chapter 1, we have Mary being told by angelic visitor that she will bear a child who will be the Son of the Most High. The problem here is that at that moment we are not told that Mary was even pregnant. Mary only recognizes that she will become pregnant with the son of God.

Let's turn next to the encounter of Mary with her cousin Elizabeth. Mary goes to visit her while Elizabeth is 6 months pregnant with the child who will become John the Baptist. Her baby leaps for joy as the baby recognizes what Mary will bring into the world. Does this make John the Baptist the first or does he tie with his mother Elizabeth since the recognition is more or less simultaneous. The problem here is once again that we really don't know if Mary was pregnant yet at that point.

Recognizing the Messiah – Other Encounters

We suppose at some point that Mary may still make claim for acknowledgement of Jesus as the Christ immediately after the birth. Let's just say for now, though, that such was never mentioned in the scriptures. But the birth of Jesus may be another place for our consideration. We are told in Luke right after the birth of Jesus that the shepherds were informed of the birth of the baby who is the Christ. Later in the same second chapter of Luke we will see the devout Simeon acknowledge what he was promised. Namely that he would not die until he had seen the Christ. Shortly thereafter we have the 84 year old prophetess, Anna, accenting the birth of Jesus, although she does not make a connection with Jesus as the Messiah or Christ.

Those of course, are all pre adult interactions outside of the brief mention of the John the Baptist encounters which do have a bold declaration, but not necessarily a Messiah or Christ statement. So let us turn to the adult interactions and recognitions of Jesus as the Christ or even as God. First let's look at the only gospel which does not have the great profession of Peter, namely the gospel of John. Here we have 3 passages to look at. The first comes in chapter 4 almost as the most dramatic passage diametrically opposed in image to the preceding chapter where we have the great religious teacher Nicodemus who has some very serious dialogue with Jesus that culminates in the famous John3:16. Later in that chapter we get a fairly strong statement from John the Baptist that he was sent as a forerunner of the Christ. There he makes many of other very bold proclamations. We may naturally read those as referencing Jesus, but we really can only make that connection in hindsight.

Chapter 4 of John gives us a fairly clear contender though. There we have the story of the Samaritan woman at the well that Jesus asks to pour a cup of water. We have detailed this story elsewhere. For here we suffice to say that it is the earliest clear expression of the adult Christ to another adult that he is indeed the Christ in the Gospel of John. We mention also briefly the passage in the eighth chapter of John where Jesus uses the I Am statement to show that he and God are one at a time when he was confronted by a religious group that references Abraham.

For our final story from the gospel of John we turn to the death of Lazarus found in chapter 11. There we find that Martha is a little critical of Jesus because she believes that he could have prevented her brother Lazarus' death. Whatever our impression is of Martha as being the one who Jesus criticizes as not making the best choice of "listening" in another story, there is still a healthy volley between Jesus and Martha in regards to the resurrection. This culminates in the recognition then Jesus is the resurrection and the life as well as the Christ. Accordingly it is actually a bolder statement by Martha than Peter makes in his great profession found in the three synoptic Gospels.

Unfortunately we do not have the great profession by Peter found in the gospel of John and therefore cannot directly determine who made this bold profession first. What we do know is that the Gospel of Mark and the Gospel of Luke have a story of an adult that precedes the great profession of Peter which recognizes Jesus as the same as God. We find in the fifth chapter of Mark as well as the eighth chapter of Luke the story of the healing of a demon possessed man.

In both gospels the man who is healed begs to go with Jesus. Instead Jesus instructs him to return to his own environment and tell others what God has done for the man. The story concludes with the understanding that the man did just that except that he told everyone how much Jesus had done for him. Given that Jesus did not make that claim directly to the man, the healed wild man came to the conclusion himself then Jesus and God were the same. This makes this the first clear recognition of an adult recognizing Jesus as either the Christ, the Messiah, or God himself, in the synoptic gospels.

Our point in this exercise is not to stir up some unsolvable debate about who the first to recognize the true identity of Jesus was. Nor is it to in anyway diminish the expression of profession made by Simon Peter. Rather it is to explore the role of innocence or naivety in a baby or a virgin. It is to acknowledge the role that women played that may have been overshadowed. It is to acknowledge that a forgiven wild man may have as much recognition as a prophet in the wilderness. It is to acknowledge the role of the foreigner, and a sinner, and a woman who was forgiven much all come together in the story of the woman at the well. You have to love how the gospels put it all together in hidden gems.

Rabbi Jesus

The term rabbi is used for Jesus on a number of occasions in a variety of contexts. One of the earliest situations occurs in the first chapter of the gospel of John. In verse 38 two disciples of John the Baptist address Jesus as rabbi and ask where he is staying. We naturally questions this because the disciples of John were certainly used to some harsh conditions. Were they curious that somebody who was given a higher stature by their own leader might have an easier life or did they even consider that perhaps even more discipline might mean that he had a more harsh lifestyle? Some of the particular significance of this is that they recognize Jesus as a rabbi before he has even taught anything.

The next reference in the gospel of John comes later in chapter 1 verse 49. By this time some of the disciples have already met Jesus and realized that he is indeed the Messiah or Christ. These disciples in turn report this to Nathaniel who has his doubts that anything good could come out of Nazareth where Jesus is reportedly from. When Jesus uses his clairvoyance to describe Nathaniel to a T, Nathaniel declares that Jesus is the son of God and addresses him as Rabbi.

We will continue our exploration with Jesus and his rabbi name by continuing to walk through the Gospel of John. Indeed this gospel might be called the rabbi gospel because over half of the references to Jesus as rabbi occur in this one gospel. The next reference occurs in the third chapter of the gospel of John and is the story of Nicodemus coming to Jesus in secret. The significance of this is that Nicodemus himself is described by Jesus as a teacher of Israel. Of course Nicodemus recognizes that as a higher rabbi Jesus has information and wisdom that would be beneficial for himself. Following this introduction and challenge we have the famous statement in John chapter 3 verse 16 where Jesus says that God so loved the world that he gave his one and only son that whoever believes in him shall not perish but have eternal life.

We next turn to some references of protection and concern offered up by the disciples to Jesus even as they address him as a rabbi. For the first such story we turn to the fourth chapter of John in which the disciples have apparently gone into town in order to get something to eat for themselves and for Jesus. In the meantime Jesus has had an encounter with the Samaritan woman to whom Jesus has revealed her past while discussing the living water of both the present and the future. Jesus makes one of his own first personal disclosures to this woman that he is indeed the Messiah whom she has referenced. Following this the disciples have now returned and urged Jesus to eat something by addressing him as rabbi. He then points out that he has already been nourished by doing God's will and God's mission.

Stephen Harrison and Richard Huizinga

Rabbi Jesus and the Disciples

We continue our discussion about Jesus as rabbi with the disciples in the protection role. The setting is once again in the gospel of John this time in chapter 11. A good friend of Jesus by the name of Lazarus has become seriously ill. The apparent delay of Jesus is an opportunity to go while Lazarus is still alive and heal him because he is after all informed of the illness while Lazarus is still alive and then he hesitates. Following that delay Jesus says to his disciples let us go back to Judaea which is where Lazarus was now residing in the tomb.

Collectively the disciples call Jesus rabbi and remind him that the Jewish leaders just tried to stone him there recently and question his notion to return there. The disciples can neither understand the mission of Jesus or his metaphors about Lazarus until he puts it in plain language. This is the sign of a good teacher or rabbi. They use symbolism and metaphors but are willing to use plain language to convey their point if nothing else works.

Most of us have heard the aphorism that there is no such thing as a dumb question which is what most good teachers try to convey. However there may be such a thing as the wrong question which displays the students as adept or, in this case, disciples who lack full appreciation on what question to frame. Consider once again the gospel of John in chapter 6. Jesus has just performed a major miracle by feeding 5000 people. Understandably that miraculous performance has people wanting him to be made king and the actual statement is listed that they intended to come and make him king by force.

Jesus had no more desire to be made an earthly king by people then he did by Satan, having already turn down that offer. He therefore withdraws by himself. The disciples go a separate route and end up in trouble on a lake. When other people discovered that he was on the other side to ask him "rabbi when did you get here?" The question should more appropriately have been how did he get there as opposed to when did he get there. However that consideration of framing the question is not even on the radar for those involved.

The disciples however can ask difficult and appropriate questions as occurs in the 9th chapter of the John. There we have the story of Jesus healing the blind man who had been blind from birth. Basically his disciples are asking a question about the connection between sin and physical illness. They are also indirectly raising the question about possible reincarnation. After all, they are asking Jesus, "rabbi who sinned, this man or his parents that he was born blind?"

Jesus does not dismiss this type of question as ignorant but points out that the man is basically there in his compromised state so that the light of the world may give "the light and sight to blind humanity." Interestingly in the Gospel of Mark chapter 11 we will have a story where Jesus asks a blind man what he would like him to do. There upon the blind man says very simply Rabbi, I want to see. There we have the most basic obvious question leading to a very simple desired result. It does not get much more straightforward than that.

We turn to another reference in the gospel of John where a simile for rabbi is used for Jesus. We understand that the meaning of rabbi is one of special teacher. In this regard we see the overlap with the term doctor which arises from the Latin docere which means to teach. And John chapter 13 we have the very humbling story of Jesus washing the feet of his disciples. After this experience he tells them that you call him teacher in the Lord which is a good thing but that they too should wash each other's feet symbolically speaking. Elsewhere in Matthew chapter 23 he warns them not to relish the title of rabbi like some religious leaders do but to recognize that they have only one true teacher.

While Jesus certainly did not appear to necessarily relish the title of the rabbi, he did seem to wear it well even perhaps when the disciples were trying to foster additional elements with that title. Such an example occurs at the mundane level after Jesus has cursed a fig tree that later dies. Peter notices this and says "rabbi, the fig tree you cursed has withered" as though this might be something major compared to what Peter has already witnessed two chapters earlier in Mark chapter 9.

There Peter has been on the mount of Transfiguration with his famous hosts. He seems perhaps a little overwhelmed and says "Rabbi let's build three Tabernacles" in order to signify the presence of Moses and Elijah along with Jesus. We even have the mention of this in parentheses that Peter was frightened and did not know what to say. Perhaps flattering our teachers when we are frightened is a thing that might turn out well for us.

Some Concluding Observations On Rabbi

Our discourses leave only a few references of the term rabbi for us to consider. We have just mentioned it only to connect with Peter but surprisingly to many people Judas has three references. Two of these references are the same story one found it in Mark chapter 14 and the other in Matthew chapter 26 where he betrays Jesus with a kiss but at the same time he calls him rabbi. Prior to this Judas has asked Jesus at the last supper in seemingly all sincerity, surely it is not I, Rabbi who will betray you, also found in Matthew chapter 26. We have addressed the story of Judas elsewhere, but these references of rabbi do indeed seem sincere.

This leads us to the only reference found after the resurrection. While many people come to ultimately recognize Jesus after the resurrection, it is only Mary who calls him rabbi after the resurrection. This seems to complete the circle of description of the term rabbi for Jesus throughout the Gospels. In summary we see that Jesus was recognized as a teacher even before he began to teach. We see both the rich and the poor addressing Jesus as Rabbi. We see the religious leaders and the blind addressing Jesus as Rabbi. We see both his enemies and his close friends using the term rabbi and likely neither of them understanding it fully. We see that we may sometimes use the term rabbi out of awe but that we should not fear asking our ill conceived questions to the one true rabbi.

Who Do People Say That I Am Versus What I Am

Who do people say that I am? That is the question raised by Jesus and recorded in Matthew chapter 16 along with Mark chapter 8 and Luke chapter 9. Christians often use the simple but definitive answer to the question by Jesus and responded to my Simon Peter that Jesus is the Messiah the son of the living God. Jesus further goes on to point out that this response by Peter was not revealed by flesh and blood but by the heavenly father. A commission is the given for Simon Peter and also a rejoinder to the disciples not to tell anyone that Jesus was the Christ or Messiah.

The origins of this question and that acknowledgement by Peter must be traced back to chapter 14 of them Matthew at the start of the chapter where John the Baptist is beheaded by King Herod. Then Jesus performs the feeding of the 5000 after he has withdrawn to a private place. The disciples meanwhile were trying to protect the privacy of Jesus as well as feed the multitudes even though the disciples had no resources. Jesus is not content with the privacy that he sought nor is he content with having people go without food. He then performs in the miracle of feeding the 5000 only to follow that up with walking on water. Jesus is effectively saying I am someone who seeks privacy and solitude but I am not certain who is attracted to that position.

There is then the interlude in chapter 15 or Jesus points out where Jesus points out that what defiles a person comes from the heart as he tries to make a statement to put in perspective for the Pharisees and religious teachers. Once again after this encounter Jesus withdraws only to be tracked down by a foreign woman who will go to whatever link it takes do you have her daughter healed. Jesus will give her a statement that the woman will argue with and win her case and be acknowledged for her faith. Jesus is effectively saying that I am someone who can be challenged and have their mission reinterpreted.

Following this, Jesus while feeding another multitude, this time of 4000 people, will be asked, amazingly, by after this by the religious leaders for a sign from heaven in regards to the "authority of Jesus". Jesus points out by analogy that they really do not know how to read signs. Then he makes his comparison after his great feedings on two occasions of multitudes by precautioning people about the yeast of the religious leaders.

Now we have the background for Jesus asking his own disciples in private who do people say I am. We must not picture Jesus as someone interested in a Facebook type of opinion. Jesus has after all already made his *I am* statement. I am someone who values the welfare and well-being of people even at the cost of my own solitude. I am one who is open to being challenged about his mission and extending that mission to the outcast and foreigners and women. I am one who challenges people who are looking for signs and claiming to be religious.

We must however continue to the story in order to see the rest of the important identity that Jesus is trying to communicate. He will proceed to point out that he is not John the Baptist and he is not Elijah or another prophet when he appears with Elijah and Moses shortly after on the transfiguration mountain. Right before that Jesus will have to rebuke no less than Peter who has made the great profession but cannot stand to hear Jesus say that he will suffer at the hands of the religious leaders and be killed.

Jesus is pointing out that *I am* not just a miracle worker. *I am* not just another prophet or John the Baptist. *I am* a suffering servant prepared to make the ultimate sacrifice. Jesus did not want it revealed to the public that he was the Messiah until people understood that suffering was involved as well as servitude and challenging the leaders of the community.

In summary *I am* someone who values connectivity over privacy. *I am* someone who values the well being of others over my own needs of the moment. *I am* someone who challenges people in the margins but includes them against the persuasions of people in power. *I am* someone who is willing to suffer at the hands of the powerful if that is what it takes for people to see a deeper meaning of life and death.

Who Do People Say That I Am – Closing Question

The question in all this identity searching is who gets who Jesus really is. We get the obvious people who don't get it. The religious leaders don't get that Jesus is the Christ, the great *I Am*. The multitudes don't get that Jesus is the Christ and not just a convenient miracle worker. We think Peter gets it because he has the succinct on the spot profession of faith that is platitudinous for all time. Yet Peter has to be rebuked a short while later precisely because he doesn't get it and what the cost of discipleship is. The person who gets it is the foreign woman who is seeking healing for her demon possessed daughter. She gets it because she challenges Jesus after he has metaphorically referred to her as a dog.

The culmination of all of this occurs in Matthew chapter 25 in the parable of the sheep and goats. I was hungry and you fed me.....Yes Jesus will take care of the needs of the multitudes as well. He will though at the same time challenge the conventional religious domain including his close associates who call him the Christ if they do not recognize the cost of discipleship. At the same time as becomes fully evident in Matthew 25, they must recognize the outcasts who do not go by the same banner and orientation. The foreign woman who is called a dog is representative of all of those outcasts and all of our opportunity. Who is that oppressed dog in our society today?

Sermon On The Mount & Other Basics

CHAPTER 2

Sermon on Truth

The Sermon on the Mount is such a gem that conveys so much wisdom in so many forms and with such concision. Beginning with the beatitudes, the tone is set for the listener to be prepared to have their world enlightened, challenged, and expanded. The beatitudes transition into metaphors extending the concepts of how we are to live. We are to be the salt of the earth. As such we are there to preserve the flavor. I laugh at the real live example in medicine of how we vilified salt or sodium because we made associations for years that did not march out with their conclusions.

Salt was a good thing in ancient times and it is a good thing now. But salt is there metaphorically speaking to preserve the truth, not a symbol of the truth. This distinction may be subtle and difficult to make at times, but it is very important to keep in mind. As a precautionary tale we think of those who are so sure that they and they alone have captured the word of God and have its application for all peoples for all times. They have confused the Eternal Truth with their vision of the moment. They have preserved the symbol and sacrificed the truth.

The next metaphor is that we are to be the light of the world. The light again represents truth which cannot be hidden. We can't be given a light that we hide under a basket. Our light is to shine before mankind in order that they may see our good works. This statement is troubling and counter to what we are often taught elsewhere. First it would appear that we might be showing off. Secondly we have the notion of works. There are, interestingly, people who are still hung up on the debate between works and faith.

We need to move on in this story which actually culminates much later in Matthew chapter 25 with the story of judgement separating the sheep from the goats. When did we see Christ in all his disguises? When we did works of charity without realizing it. Finally we are to recognize that we can do "good". This is word that sometimes troubles us because Jesus once asked the religious leaders why they called him "good" Master since no one was good but God alone. We may miss the point here in that Jesus is willing to sacrifice his own image or symbolism that he is good because he is a symbol for the ultimate truth.

Now some will say "wait a minute, didn't Jesus say that he was the way, the truth, and the light, and that no one can come to the father but by me. Yes. Now substitute way, truth, and light for "me" at the end of that scripture and perhaps we can see this in a new light literally.

Sermon on Anger

Now to be clear that Jesus did not come to destroy actual truth that went with historical symbols he makes the statement right after this that he has not come to destroy the law or the prophets. Rather he has come to fulfill them, which is to expand their meaning without getting caught up In their ancient literalism. Just because the Commandments have new meanings does not imply that the Commandments can actually be

Parables and Paradox

broken. We may miss the next meaning of paired challenges because of our bias and prejudice.

We next hear Jesus saying that our righteousness needs to exceed that of the religious leaders. Those were the people who knew the commandments and arguably kept them to a fairly high degree. We have references to this concept by Jesus elsewhere when he is giving another challenge to those leaders by basically saying woe to them who kept all these details but missed the heart of the command. No, the notion here is to expand the meaning, not forgo it.

So Jesus proceeds with the basic concept of anger. The old message was don't murder but the new message is don't even be angry with your brother because this is the seeds of murder sown in the heart. There is a clause though that provides that if we have a cause that perhaps our anger is ok. We will let the reader speculate what that cause was but let's say that it's safe to say that it might include measures such as anger against child molesters or some such. In other words, get angry when you see injustice wherever that injustice may be.

The next portion which is related to this appears more to the point about those whom we deal with on a day to day basis. This could be our loved ones, business associates, etc. We are admonished to go and reconcile with our fellow human beings before we can effectively worship the truth and light. This is paired with the anger notion above because Jesus understood that it was human nature to harbor and breed irritation and resentment against those that we are closest to that would turn into anger which then effectively "killed" the relationship. Good enough. But wait. We are admonished to go to the other party even if it was they who initiated what we are offended by. Read the challenge in Matthew 5:23-24 again. We are to reconcile by going to our brother or anyone else close to us simply if they have anything against us. This is not meant to be confrontational, but rather reconciliatory regardless of who is at fault.

That seems a bit much. Then the concept of reconciliation is extended to include our adversaries with rather harsh consequences if we don't reconcile. Wow.

Sermon on Transparency

Jesus proceeds to challenge conventions by taking on adultery and divorce next. This topic is sandwiched between the anger and taking an oath topics. He backs up the adultery position to the point of looking with lust as primordial (see our treatise on David and Bathsheba). Arguably even the actions before looking are a setup that is to be avoided. Maybe it's turning on the internet late at night for just a look. If your right hand causes you to sin..... if your right eye causes you to sin....Of course one can distinguish a true literalist as someone who has actually completed those sentences as Jesus described. Otherwise they are just merely selective in their choices.

This sequence is then followed by an admonition not to swear by anything but to let the words like yes and no stand for themselves. In other words, your word needs to be as strong as any contractual arrangement. This concept of oaths is tied to the legal right for paybacks when someone has been wronged.

Jesus takes this to the extreme of forgiveness by suggesting to turn the other cheek, and to go the extra mile when forced to go a lesser distance. This passive action takes the penultimate when we are to pray for our enemies and those who persecute us. God's daily gifts of rain and sunshine after all, are available to good and evil alike. If we wish to be beacons for truth, we need to distinguish ourselves by loving those who don't love us. This comes close to perfection as Jesus points out we must ultimately be.

Sermon on Priorities

It is interesting that the only editorial on the sermon on mount by Jesus is in regard to the concept of forgiveness. This seems to be at first reading that God cannot forgive us until we forgive our fellow human beings. Perhaps though an alternative explanation is that we are simply not in a mindset to accept or understand forgiveness until we have first forgiven.

This is then followed by remarks on fasting. Mind you, Jesus is not advocating against fasting, but rather that when you do fast that the attention is turned internally. This is back to the prelude where Jesus instructs people that prayer is a private event. The next statement is so simple and yet so profound where he states that where your treasure is, there will be your heart also. This is followed by the notion that you can't serve God and money.

In between those gems is back to the lamp and light imagery involved earlier, this time with the eye being the portal of entry. The concept of not worrying about money or being hung up on it is extended to not worrying about tomorrow, food and clothing in the wonderful and simplistic imagery at the conclusion of Matthew chapter 6. We are admonished to model the birds of the air and the lilies of the field when it comes to food, clothes, and tomorrow. In so doing, Jesus does point out that there will be daily troubles, but that we do not need to give any advance concern about tomorrow.

Sermon on Wisdom

As good as the imagery is in chapters 5 and 6 in the Sermon on the Mount, chapter 7 of Matthew closes on with a strong series of imagery and stories. The "be wary of judgment" message is illustrated by the picture of trying to remove a speck from our neighbor while all the while we have a log in our own. We sometimes forget that we are actually challenged to remove the log in order to remove that speck.

Next we have the challenge to keep seeking and asking as illustrated by the comparison that earthly fathers don't give their offspring stones when they ask for bread. Jesus notes that on some level that everyone who seeks will find, he who asks will be rewarded, and he who knocks will have the door opened.

Next we move to the imagery of entering the kingdom by the narrow gate. There are shades of this elsewhere when Jesus says it's easier to go through the eye of a needle than for a rich man to enter the kingdom. Here though the concept is broadened to anyone whose life is dominated by material possessions. Of course, at some level we are all judged by the fruit that we bear. This is not in contradistinction to the admonition and precautions earlier about judging. We do judge by the fruits of actions ultimately, not by any or all of the theories, creeds or symbols that stand between the fruit and the truth.

Jesus closes with arguably the only true parable in the Sermon on the Mount where the wise man built his house on the solid rock as opposed to the foolish man who built on the shifting sand. The imagery is simple but it is again all predicated on both listening and putting into action. "Whoever hears these words of mine and puts them into practice, is like a wise man....

In summary the Sermon on the Mount begins with attitudes and perspectives that are desirable. There are specific actions that we are admonished to perform that are not necessarily conventional but do bear fruit. These perspectives will be repeated throughout the gospels, especially through parables.

Parables and Paradox

Sermon on Priorities (The Challenge of Being Human)

We must confess that when we read the conclusion of chapter 6 of Matthew that we are challenged by our own human nature. After all Jesus begins the 25th verse of Matthew chapter 6 by instructing us to not worry about our lives including such basics as what we will eat or drink or what we will wear. Then he makes this wonderful comparisons to the birds of the air who don't sew or reap along with the metaphor of the lilies of the field who don't toil or spin.

Our first reading of this passage needs us to be humbled by these very natural measures that do not worry but have an acceptance that God provides. This of course is not something that they have a choice in. They can not choose to be worry free or care free or for the other side of the coin to be full of worry. The distinction with human beings is that they indeed have a choice as to whether to worry or to trust in a source that will ultimately provide the essentials.

This session is rather about establishing values and priorities. First there is a recognition by Jesus that food and clothing and drink are essential for life. We read in verse 32 that the heavenly father knows that we need all of these measures. He simply asked us to establish a priority of seeking the kingdom and the righteousness as our top priority. By doing so we will have access in a worry free fashion as we were designed to have.

The conclusion of the chapter as well as the conclusion of the section give legitimate due to the troubles of each day. Jesus closing statement is that each day has enough trouble of its own. We are to focus our energy and efforts on the priorities of the day in order to have an enriched live in the Now moment. Right before this we are told that tomorrow will worry about itself which is somewhat of a paradox for all of this section that seemingly begins by instructing us how to not worry.

The reality is that we cannot only not deny our human nature but that we are instructed to use our sensory perceptions in order to process our legitimate needs in ways that nature cannot do. We are not called to some impossible task of Zen meditation. Rather we are told to consider nature and to reflect on it. We are to picture the birds of the air and to envision the lilies of the field. We are simply to give up our preoccupation and avoid being absorbed and consumed by these measures.

The challenge of this passage is not in asking us to do the impossible but rather to show us what is possible if we have our priorities straight. It is not a Lion King animalistic worry free philosophy. It is a very human oriented perspective that recognizes and legitimizes our daily needs. Indeed our ultimate manifestation as human beings is to reflect and ponder on life's most basic measures without becoming preoccupied or fixated or obsessed with them. This requires a divine grace and presence.

The Lord's Prayer

The model prayer we are given by the Master in the sermon on the mount is so basic and so familiar that it is easy to miss the deep and subtle messages that are buried. This elemental gem comes at the center or heart of Jesus fundamental moral Sermon on the Mount. Matthew chapter 6 begins with a reminder that our good deeds are to be done in private. So too our prayers. Both our good deeds and prayers are contrasted with religious leaders who like the public display. They already have their reward we are told which amounts to the recognition they were seeking here on earth.

Meanwhile, those who are seeking a deeper reward are instructed to do things in private for a better reward. This includes praying. Paradoxically when we pray in private we are immediately united with other believers. This is evidenced by Jesus first word "our". If we are praying in private and are instructed to begin with our, there must be some unifying element that brings a collective awareness to the process. We align our spirits in basic beliefs about a higher power.

Next we are instructed to honor God's name. There are many names employed for God but when Jesus is illustrating his most basic connection with God he uses the ancient "I Am". The believer is then instructed to pray that God's will be done on earth as it is in heaven. This implies that God's will is already being done somewhere and that again we are to align with that will. After recognizing the honor of name there is the recognition that God is king and the request that God's kingdom come on earth as it is in heaven.

We see that the formula is to begin with recognizing unity. Then there is the importance of recognizing the essential power and honor of being. Next we see that we are to request aligning with that essential power. After we have achieved that triad then we are empowered to tell God what to do. The first command we give is a blend where we request that God's will be done as it is in heaven. Immediately then we tell God to give us our daily bread. No matter what version is employed here the emphasis is practical and on basic human needs.

This food command is the first of the three F's: food, forgiveness, and forgoing trials. There is a demand for forgiveness but it tied to ourselves forgiving others. Forgiveness means letting go of our preoccupation with offense. We cannot have a peace of mind that comes with forgiveness unless we have let go of the offenses that we are carrying. The original Aramaic emphasizes being serene while allowing other their serenity. The final command to God is that we forgo trials by getting protection from the evil one. The Message adds the command to keep us safe from ourselves and the Devil.

Stephen Harrison and Richard Huizinga

The Ego and The Lord's Prayer

It is easy for us to be misled by the introduction to the Lord's Prayer if we do not realize that the challenges and admonitions which proceeded are meant as much for ourselves as they were to the people that they seem to be directed at, namely the religious leaders of that time. Chapter 6 of Matthew begins with a warning to the ego about caution of doing our work or acts of righteousness in order to be recognized by people. This gives us a chance for a true reward from God in heaven.

Perhaps we are so eager to get to the part about the hypocrites and the religious leaders that we skip over the next section. The next section is a presumption by Jesus that we will actually be giving to the needy. It is said so succinctly that perhaps it almost goes without notice. Indeed that's exactly what Jesus wants us to do is to give as though it is natural with no ego involved and not needing to demonstrate before others but rather to do so in secret without ego and be recognized by God.

Next comes a stronger admonition for us and specifically what to avoid. There we are told to avoid being like the hypocrites who love to pray standing in the synagogue and on street corners in order to be seen. Perhaps we have translated all these years that hypocrites are automatically the religious leaders of that time. However we would have to make that extrapolation from other scriptures in order to derive that. Indeed we are actually told to not be like the pagans who have many babbling words.

Then Jesus delivers his gem which we have entitled the Lord's Prayer. Once again this prayer is devoid of ego and opens up with the word "our". Recognition and honor is given to God and his name and his kingdom. It is his will which is to be done and not our own and certainly not mine. The blessings also our collective blessings in which it is give us our daily bread and forgive us our debts and to lead us not into temptation. It is all us. No I, no me.

Then Jesus returns once again to acts of personal action. Yes we are to fast but we are not to have our ego in the fasting for appearance sake. Rather we are to look our best so that our God who sees beyond our ego will reward us. Next Jesus is very aware that the ego would store up for itself treasures on earth but instead he challenges us to store up treasures in heaven where there is no destruction. After all where our treasure is will be our heart also.

Jesus closes the sixth chapter of Matthew by showing us what happens when nature removes the ego. The ego is full of worry including what we eat and drink and what we wear and perhaps whether or not we should have some cosmetic surgery. Jesus pointed out that the birds in the air don't sow or reap or worry but that they have enough to eat. So too do the flowers in the fields neither labor or spin and yet their natural beauty exceeds even the greatest that history has seen.

Cost Value Options

The Cost of Discipleship as told by Jesus seems Strident and Stringent at first reading. The emphasis is on Cost and Hate. And there is no clear description of Discipleship, that being left to our assumption or a prior telling. What we are left with is an extreme picture and a curious one if the description was meant to enhance recruitment to Jesus' world of Discipleship. The question we're left with is, "Who would want to be a Disciple?" And why?

When Jesus references Discipleship, it seems to point to the Sermon on the Mount. The list of traits portrayed there point to a life of worship first and then sacrifice for the benefit of others. Even the Beatitudes describe persona who most of us would never describe as "blessed". Yet Christ does, despite the popular perception that the Beatitude folks are downtrodden (their fault), weak, or wasting their time on heavenly notions.

Much of the rest of the Sermon deals with self sacrifice to benefit others, (all examples of no retribution to right wrongs) or sincere worship without the flourish and drama rendered by priests and their ilk.

The desired reaction to events in a life, especially negative events, are counter to reasonable expectations of protection, retribution or disappointment. Instead we are told to turn the other cheek, forgive debts or wrongs, and go out or way to help our enemies.

Jesus' cost equation is reversed from the norm. Jesus demands we give up spending time, energy and money to acquire normal society values of wealth, family or social relationships, and honor.

The traditional cost/ value formula demands what we spend should provide value that exceeds cost. The question we ask usually, "Was it worth it"? And if the answer is "Yes", we feel placated, at ease, "life is good". And then start another cycle when the thrill is gone.

Not so with Jesus. He demands we give up gain and work so that others benefit and gain. We want the glory of the transfiguration, but not the work of the wilderness, prayer and fasting. We wish to be included with the sheep, but we want to be selective to whom we dispense our good works. Jesus' cost/value paradigm cedes our earthly benefit to the needy, the bully, the bad egg, while we are left to deal with the mess. Not fair, you shout?

Maybe not. Yet, our reward is in heaven; in return, here on earth, we avoid sinking to the depths of those who return evil for evil, who employ power for greed, who look for satisfaction in all the wrong places.

God and Ambiguity

Embrace ambiguity. That is the unwritten, unspoken, yet subtly implied lesson hidden in the Sermon On The Mount in Mattew chapter 6. There we have the model prayer for which we must keep in mind the background. We are instructed to pray in private or secret with the strong implication that this is a personal and private adventure. This makes the first word "our" stand out all the more. If it is a private process, who are the others invoked by the word our? This implies a unity with others that cannot be explained by the physical absence of others.

So too is our first inclination to think of others as implied by the term us used several times later. Give us our daily bread, forgive us our debts, do not tempt us, deliver us from evil. Every phrase here is not a request to God without a polite please attached. Rather it is a direct command to God. Jesus is effectively telling us to tell God what to do.

But buried in that third us command is not only the command to not be put to the test coupled with the fear implied, but also the suggestion that somehow God is involved in the temptation as the tempter or at least the tester. Is there an implication that God contains both good and evil? Is this a leftover of a dualistic God?

We assume that the us refers to other believers who are not present consistent with the opening word "our". But, is that all it can mean? What if at least one the uses of us refers to the team of God and the person praying? Some of these combinations don't seem to work well with God being the other party, but that may be because of our preexisting bias. We simply don't wish to think that God could be either tempted or be the one doing the tempting. But ambiguity allows for that.

Stephen Harrison and Richard Huizinga

Simple Prayers

When it comes to prayer, Jesus liked things to be simple. Look at his own model prayer found in Matthew chapter 6 on the Sermon on the Mount. As we note elsewhere, the first word of that prayer begins with "our". We are united first by recognizing something not only greater than ourselves, but something that unites us with others who are not even present, who may not belong to the same denomination, or even wear the banner of Christian. While we then recognize the respect that God commands, we utter this phrase your will be done on earth as it is in heaven. This seems like a tautology of sorts until we realize that a God, who honors free will, can only have his will done on earth by people who are firmly entrenched in the earth.

Furthermore, we can only do that will when we have had our physical needs met by receiving our daily bread. We then deliver that good will to others in the physical sense to the unknown disguises of Jesus in Matthew 25 in the sheep and goats parable. Maybe even the undeserving. When did we see him? That is another of the simple prayers that Jesus illustrates in that parable. Our actions are to be done on behalf of our fellow human beings because of their daily needs, not because they wear a designation of Christian.

We turn to a few other simple prayers that Jesus illustrates in the gospels. Recall the story of Pharisee and the tax collector in Luke chapter 18 who had their respective prayers. After the ostentatious prayer by the religious authority, the tax collector beats his breast and says "God, be merciful to me, a sinner." Effectively, there are 4 active words in that prayer: God, Mercy, me, sinner. The existentialist statement is that God is Mercy. Humans are sinners. But sinners are empowered to tell God what to do. Give us our bread, forgive us, etc. This is the same type of reward seen in the widow and the unjust judge. She is rewarded for her belief and persistence.

In Luke chapter 23 we have the story of the thief on the cross. He rebukes his fellow thief who like the crowd, mocks Jesus. Jesus only acknowledges the man when the man says first to Jesus "remember me". That simple prayer or supplication is rewarded with instant paradise. Ask and you shall receive, as Matthew chapter 7 admonishes. Jesus own simple prayer at his height of his anguish is, if possible, let this cup pass. Nonetheless, not my will but your will be done.

These prayers are framed by doing God's will. They are not presumptive that we ever understand God's will, but rather if we are persistent in our efforts for self and fellow humans, we will be recognized and remembered and rewarded. Under the circumstances, we may never understand God's will, but we can still do it.

Sermon on The Mount Introductory Commands

The sermon on the mount is framed by measures that are implied commands though they are not direct commands. Jesus begins by giving a series of blessings known as the beatitudes which implies a command to be a certain way. He closes the sermon with a parable about the wise man who built his house on the rock as compared to the foolish man who built his house on the sand. The implication just to have a solid foundation as our place of refuge. Neither of these frames is a direct command although the sermon itself has many direct commands. We are, however told to rejoice when others have great rewards, to maim ourselves, to fast, to actually remove the metaphorical speck from someone else's eye, look at nature, let others who are abusing us abuse us some more, love our enemies and do other unnatural measures. So let's take a look at the actual statements.

The first actual command comes after the blessings for the beatitudes. We are told to rejoice when others give us harsh treatment and persecution on the account of the gospel because our reward in heaven will be great. The next command comes in Matthew five verse 16 earlier told by the master to let our light shine before men in order that they may see our good deeds. The next command is one not to think that Jesus has come not to abolish the law or Original Testament but rather that we are to surpass the righteousness of the leaders of his day. We are lulled in to commands that we want to hear: be good to get a reward, show off our good deeds, and better the hypocritical leaders. Well and good.

Now that we have been pulled into to the desired position it's about to become a little more challenging. Jesus is going to show us exactly how to exceed the legitimate righteousness of the religious leaders by not merely avoiding murder, but commanding us to not be angry with our fellow human beings or to even call them fools. Then we are told to reconcile with our fellow human beings even when we are not at fault before we can worship properly. We are to settle grievances before court even if we are not the offending party.

Next Jesus shows us once again how to exceed the Original Testament commands of not committing adultery. We are to cut off our hand and to pluck out our eye if these cause us to sin. Seems pretty harsh for even a metaphor. But after he has our attention with these harsh metaphors, he is going to bring it back to both the Original Testament and an extension of it. No one is to divorce their wife unless their is unfaithfulness because this produces adultery. Now we have all heard plenty of conservative Christian camps preach against homosexuality and gender identity about which Jesus said nothing, compared to these days the silence on divorce about which he gave explicit commands.

But in case we and Jesus have not offended those who bash orientation let's look at his words again. Mind you these are his words in his most basic instructions and not ours. Jesus quotes that anyone who divorces his wife must give her a certificate of divorce. Again he does not refute this statement but rather elaborates on it. Once again notice exactly what he does say and specifically what he does not.

In the divorce statement that Jesus endorses, we must be careful to avoid anachronistic moralism. This section is meant to protect women. Divorce is meant to be avoided for inconvenience and whimsical reasons. We believe that the admonition against marrying a divorced woman ties in to the earlier statement of unchastity. In other words, to connect with an unchaste woman is the same type of adultery that Jesus talks about when looking at a woman with lust.

Sermon on The Mount – Be Authentic

Now we continue with the commands that are once again seldom preached upon. In Matthew chapter 5 Jesus commands us to not swear. He is once again extending the Original Testament enjoinder to keep our oath. He notes that we are not to swear by heaven, earth, our bodies, etc. Rather, we are to let our affirmations and statements be simply yes or no. To be sure we understand that Jesus is not telling us to avoid swearing in the vulgar sense. We suppose this combination of commands does not preclude the statement "Hell yes" since swearing by hell was not prohibited. This section of commands rather allows us to simply affirm our existential being. Are we a Christian, are we oriented a certain way, are we a certain political persuasion. We do not strengthen the position of any particular process when we appeal to God or even "the Bible says".

Next we move from the earlier commands to actively maim ourselves in order to avoid sin to passively allowing someone else to harm us. After the Orginal Testament eye for eye standard is invoked, Jesus tells us to turn the other cheek after we have been stricken. If someone sues us, give them the shirt off our back. If we are forced to bear a burden, then extend the service. Give to whoever asks us. No reference to means testing. To demonstrate that he means to extend the old guard to extremism, Jesus tells us to not only love our enemies, but to pray for those who persecute us. This is specifically paired with becoming sons of God the Father. This section, along with the chapter concludes with its final command, to be perfect as our Heavenly Father.

The next chapter of Matthew,6, begins with the command to to do righteousness for its own sake and not for the reward of our contemporaries. We are to continue giving to the needy, regardless of means testing. In fact we are to do this so naturally that our own body won't even know. This performance of charitable acts in secret is the prelude to praying in secret which itself is the introduction to The Lord's Prayer. We have discussed elsewhere the subtlety directly stated in that prayer about commands. Within the most compact Prayer we are commanded to give which is right at the heart of the commands in the Sermon on the Mount.

We now are given a series of statements that we are to command God to do. Your kingdom comes with "your" will, give us our daily bread, forgive our debts, lead us not into temptation but deliver us from evil.

Next we are told to not mistake the pairing of fasting with public display of solemnity. In fact, fasting is assumed to be an act of worship, reflection, or contrition. We are only told how to do it, namely with the same face that we always have such that is secret or private. The section closes with us receiving the command to not store treasures on earth but rather in heaven where our hearts should be and the treasures are eternal. To make sure that we do not displace the eternal with the temporal, we are commanded to be like the birds of the air and the lilies of the field by not worrying. We are told to get our priorities straight by seeking the kingdom of the Heavenly Father and his righteousness and to not focus on the worries of tomorrow which are inevitably expressions of lack of faith.

Sermon on The Mount – The Golden Rule

Chapter 7 of Matthew begins with a seemingly simple command to not judge. Then it implies not only that we will, being human, continue to judge and have that same standard that is in our heart applied to ourselves until we stop judging people who are of course, not like ourselves. Yet we are to help others by assisting them in extricating even the minor faults that they possess. How is this seeming paradox possible? It's all right there. We are to remove the log in our own eye in order to remove the speck from our fellow human being. Medically speaking, those who have ever struggled to remove a tiny speck from someone's eye realize that it is often easier to remove something much larger. Immediately following this is the command to not throw our pearls before swine or to give our sacred wisdom to dogs. People with minor impairment must desire to see better in order for us to spend our time on their imperfections.

Next we have the simplicity that is both a command from Jesus and at the same time instructions for us to demand the basics from God much the same way as the subtleties of the Lord's Prayer in the preceding chapter. Ask. Seek. Knock. All have a reward. So as not to miss that this reward is meant to be from our Heavenly Father, Jesus points out that God will not be outdone by our earthly fathers. We have, however, moved from the very much physical nature of bread in the Lord's Prayer, to something much more spiritual. This concept is paired immediately with the Golden rule, which not only summarizes the entire Old Testament, but also is to be a summary of our daily lives.

Enter the narrow gate we are told next. Not narrow minded. Rather we are challenged to focus on the essentials rather than on the elaborate schematic that corporate religion is often ensconced in. This is followed by the notion to watch out for false prophets. We take great pride in knowing that we could identify such except that we are meant to realize that they may be right in our midst with the same spiritual clothing, creeds, denominations, etc. Jesus wishes to make this connection abundantly clear by noting that such people will even point out that they prophesied, drove out demons, and performed miracles in the name of Jesus. The rejection of such individuals is a prelude to the parable in Matthew chapter 25 about the sheep and goats and the many disguises of Jesus. This command of Jesus is the last command in the Sermon on The Mount and is meant to represent the last judgement as does the sheep and goats separation. We separate ourselves by doing charitable acts in private to others who may be as far different from us in their orientation and perspective as they can be.

Being And Doing

The Beatitudes found in Matthew chapter 5 are an existential statement of how we are to be. They are fairly straightforward, but some of the idioms may not be preserved as intended over time. For example, what does it mean to be poor in spirit? Is it a type of humble recognition that keeps us being to full of our own spirit? Is it small spirit compared to big Spirit? Our purpose in this section is not to do an exegesis on what such verbiage would mean today, but rather how it intersects with Matthew chapter 25 in the story where the sheep are separated from the goats.

In so doing a smash up of these 2 teachings, we will take some liberties here. Blessed are those who mourn, for they will be comforted. This mourning could be about any of the deprivations experienced by the recipients in the sheep and goats story. Blessed are the meek, for they will inherit the earth. We often hear of mean being interpreted as disciplined. Certainly one has to be disciplined to do the good works in the sheep and goats story if you are continually serving the lowliest of life without knowing who they are and what kind of reward they will receive.

Blessed are those who hunger and thirst for righteousness, for they will be filled. This hunger and thirst is not to be confused with the literal hunger and thirst seen in the sheep and goats story. Rather, it is a continuous search to search how we are to serve, even when we think we already know. The merciful will receive mercy. Extending mercy by definition implies aid to someone undeserving.

Next we have the daunting task of being pure in heart in order to see God. Good luck with that. Except the sheep do get to see God by virtue of their good work that they did without knowing who they were helping. Closely related are the peacemakers who get to be called sons of God. People who seek harmony despite seeming ideological differences.

Blessed are the persecuted because of righteousness, for theirs is the kingdom of heaven. Squaring this up with the sheep and goats we see that we may indeed be persecuted for helping the least of these because they don't look and act like us. It is only a slight change to render this concept of blessed are you when you persist in helping the afflicted and misunderstood as blessed are you when you are persecuted by the self righteous.

Social Justice and The Sermon on the Mount

Jesus next warns us about storing up too much capital on this earth we are naturally people who don't have such reserve will want to break in and steal. But he does not condone the stealing he does recognize that this is one of the inevitable outcomes of inequity. Inequity is associated with iniquity. Next he points out that the lens we look at to see life with determines literally how we view life. If we are looking through the lens of darkness and hatred and bigotry and injustice then our darkness is indeed great.

Next Jesus gives a challenge to the people present who have enough to eat and enough to wear and to not be so consumed about this process. Such people worry about tomorrow and what the stock market will do to their 401K and forget about the mission that life has given each of them to do today. When we seek the kingdom of heaven with all its righteousness and justice then we can appreciate these things for not only ourselves but for those who may not enjoy such basics of life.

Jesus then has some stern words beginning in Matthew chapter 7 for those who judge others. He recognized that often such people in a position to judge picked on rather trivial matters while ignoring their own major offenses. Surely he could not have been talking about the economic exploitation of a large group of people being taking advantage of as a major offense. Nonetheless he was making the strong connection that it was not obvious to those who sat in the judgment seat.

Indeed we are asked to remove the plank from our eyes that is analogous to the oppressive foot on the neck. Jesus then again becomes the voice for the disenfranchised when he tells us to ask and it will be given to us, to seek and we will find, and to knock and the door will be opened. When a group of people asks for social justice and seeks social justice and knocks on the door for social justice it is expected that such will occur. Is it any wonder that they will return to the demand concept in the Lord's Prayer if they are denied basics that are their inherent right?

Jesus will close the Sermon on the Mount with a series of challenges that include the golden rule of doing to others what you would have them do to you which he points out is a summation of the entire Original Testament. He goes on to point out that using his name cannot be a substitution for practicing the will of God which includes compassion for those in need as summarized in Matthew chapter 25 on the day of judgment.

A Higher Law From the Sermon on the Mount

There is both danger and appropriateness in turning to scripture to find directions and answers for the challenges that life brings. This process may naturally lend itself to a distortion of the original scripture in a way that becomes a sort of sanctified destruction of the original meaning. With that in mind, we will attempt to address the issue of racial imbalance with the Sermon on the Mount including the Lord's Prayer. In so doing we recall the words of Lincoln during the civil war that both sides prayed to the same God.

Certainly the Beatitudes can be distorted to show that there is a blessing when you suffer and are meek and humble and therefore that we should not engage ourselves too much with suffering and injustice because perhaps such suffering is ordained because certainly it is blessed. While we can conveniently cloak such scripture with rationalization, it is harder to escape the mercy clause in Matthew chapter 5 as well as the charge to be peacemakers.

Of course our officers of the law are legally empowered with keeping the peace. So too is the rest of society by scripture. Keeping the peace by society certainly has to invoke a social justice that also insures that just as there is a law that is higher than any earthly law, that so too those who are sworn to uphold the law must answer to all of its implications. Furthermore the fact that there is a blessing for those who are persecuted and insulted is hardly a mandate to perform such atrocities.

We discover next that followers of truth are to be the salt of the earth and light of the world. Accordingly our actions are both essential for the most basic justice and also give seasoning and enhancement for lives that are bland. We cannot hide the light of justice that was given already in the Original Testament when we are told that basically all God desires of us is to walk humbly with our God and love justice. Dare we say that a peaceful protest can combine the essence of these charges.

Next Jesus is clear that he is asking for a deeper interpretation of the law from the Original Testament and not a suspension of it. He is very clear that we are to respect every aspect of the law. At the same time, we are to take the meaning of the law to a higher justice and sense than was being applied in his day. Then he challenges the most righteous of us all by basically saying that murder begins with anger and name calling. Ouch.

Now that he has our attention Jesus says next in Matthew chapter 5 that we cannot even effectively worship without reconciling with a brother that we are at odds with. Before we can offer our humble gifts of money, time, and talent, we must reconcile with those that we are at odds with. Note specifically that no mention is made of who is right or wrong here. So even if you did not commit the injustice of slavery and the aftermath of racial poverty and inequity, it is still your duty to resolve it.

Social Justice and the Sermon on the Mount Practical Advice

We might naturally ask who is our brother or a sister that Jesus is referring to in Matthew chapter 5. We look elsewhere in Matthew chapter 12 to see the answer defined clearly. In that context people were telling Jesus that his literal brothers were outside along with his mother. He pointed out that his mother and his brothers were those that did the will of his father in heaven. Now all we have to do is to define what the will of God is.

Parables and Paradox

Jesus gives very practical advice for daily application. In this context he tells people who are going to court to settle their differences for practical reasons. The judge may side with the other accuser and someone be placed in prison until they're able to pay their way out. If we apply this to today's penal system we see the obvious parallels with people placed in our prison system and a recurrence cycle because they do not have the funds to break that cycle.

Yet for those afflicted with such challenges there is still the very practical admonition to make friends so that these extreme things that perpetuate the problem do not come about. After some other practical advice, Jesus will then address the ancient struggle that we face today yet of an eye for an eye. Practically speaking, how do we apply that admonition for today's circumstances? Now Jesus has moved beyond the family concept and the friend concept to include our enemies.

Very clearly Jesus is acknowledging that people may have enemies for one reason or another. But he admonishes us to love our enemies and pray for those who persecute us in order to be part of a larger family, namely the family of God. After he has our attention with this rather extreme challenge of prayer for our enemies he then makes it more practical and applicable to today's situation. We are too greet not only our own people but we are to extend the love of God to those who are not like us.

Next Jesus is aware that it might be easy for some people to be giving a gift of money perhaps or the like if they can do it at a distance and yet receive recognition for this. And the Jesus acknowledges the reward for such as rather superficial. Secret giving for situations that we do not always know may have its own separate and higher reward. Next we are challenged with some ways to avoid praying and then a very specific model of how to pray.

The model prayer begins with the word our which signifies unity rather than division and discord. Meanwhile we are told that because God knows what we need that we don't need to ask him for measures but rather demand that we receive certain essentials. Granted the model prayer teaches us first to recognize holiness and to pray for God's will to be done on earth. Then we demand bread and forgiveness and not to be the lead in temptation but rather delivered from evil. This prayer is a demand for the basics of life coupled with a justice that exceeds earthly justice but does not ignore it.

Prosperity And The Sermon On The Mount Part One

The Sermon on the Mount does not seem to speak much about the prosperity gospel. We make assumptions that Jesus is giving his timeless statements to the crowd, most of whom were likely poor. Probably not too bold an assumption on the economic makeup of the crowd except that it is not clear from the Bible in most versions that Jesus was speaking to the crowd. Jesus goes to a mountainside and sits down. His disciples followed.

Most versions note that his teachings or sermon began after the disciples came to him. Our understanding would be that Jesus is speaking to the disciples at that point and not necessarily the crowd. Mind you, perhaps it was intended that the disciples pass this message on to the crowd at that point. Perhaps the intent was to do so at a later date. We will go with the former because at the conclusion of the sermon we read that when he finished that the crowd was amazed.

How the message of that day was communicated is of no small importance to the message of the gospel for us today. A message here is spread from the source to people of humble origin. Indeed fishermen, tax collectors and the like we are told elsewhere. We are also told elsewhere that they had sacrificed all, although in that context there seems to be an element of what's in it for me given the sacrifices that are made.

For now we will go with the premise that Jesus is speaking to a group of generally humble on the economic, essential worker types that will both understand the symbols employed and basic language. He opens with the beatitudes. The attitudes that we should be. Poor in spirit with a small s. Not full of ourselves and hung up on our egoistic thinking of what life should offer. Such folks get everything right off the bat, namely the kingdom of heaven.

Next Jesus tells these generally non affluent disciples that people are blessed if they mourn. This is not merely about suffering as we all do. Rather it is about reflecting deeply on our losses as well as on others. Regret and sadness over loss are woven into the meaning of mourning. If we want to be comforted, we must lose something. Seemingly we have gone from gaining the kingdom with the first beatitude to necessarily losing something if we want to be comforted.

Of course the astute listener then as now gets the similarities of the first 2 beatitudes. Both are simply a way of losing ourselves. Now we turn to the meek proposition. The Oxford English Dictionary notes meek to include easily imposed upon or submissive. All of this is now sounding more like the ancient Chinese Tao. The submissive only inherit the earth though compared to the poor in spirit who get the kingdom of heaven. Maybe that was practical advice for a people that had to be somewhat submissive to the Romans. Then too Jesus could not be accused of subversion to the Romans.

Prosperity And The Sermon On The Mount Part 2

The next attitude to be is to hunger and thirst for righteousness. Is this meant to be a priority test for a potentially hungry crowd? We maintain that Jesus will define in no uncertain terms what it means to be righteous later in Matthew chapter 25. There with the sheep and goats parable he brings all of this together. When we tie in the next precept of being merciful we realize that we are called to be righteous without direct or indirect means testing.

Surely Jesus must have been speaking metaphorically when he uttered his next beatitude of being pure in heart with the consequence of that behavior and perspective of actually seeing God. Given that Jesus did not come to do away with the Original Testament where no one actually ever saw God, how do we reconcile this bold assertion? Perhaps Mother Theresa captures this when she refers to seeing Christ in all his humble disguises, much again like the sheep and goats in Matthew 25.

Jesus wants us to be peacemakers. In order to do this we have to be at peace with ourselves as exemplified in the earlier precepts. They will be sons of God. To be clear, like most families, there will be differences, but the peacemakers look for the common ground and also the ability to compromise on the nonessentials. The beatitudes close in a symmetrical fashion with a reward being the kingdom of heaven for holding steadfast to the truth at the price of personal sacrifice.

The rest of the Sermon on the Mount is basically an expansion of all of these precepts. Furthermore Jesus wishes to be clear that these concepts are absolutely tied into the Original Testament teachings and are not antithetical but rather extensions. They are not subversive to the Roman system when the soldiers conscripted civilians to carry their provisions. The precepts were not antithetical to the courts of law.

Chapter 5 in Matthew represents the portion of the Sermon on the Mount that mainly deals with the relationship of the individual to society, traditional and current. Chapter 6 is about personal relationships. The Lord's Prayer is given as a private matter. So is the concept of fasting. We are instructed to store up treasures in heaven and not worry about even the basics of life such as food and clothing.

Measures culminate in chapter 7 where basically we are told not to judge others who may have another value system of values or beliefs. We ultimately get what we seek and ask for. This is not the modern prosperity gospel but rather the application of ancient principles. That is why it is so fundamentally imperative to have attitudes that the whole diatribe began with. We all get what we ask for. This was not news. Rather it was the simplicity combined with elegant visions that was unique.

The Really Offensive Gospel

CHAPTER 3

Prelude and overview of the Major Offenses

The parable of the talents is one of those offensive stories in the gospel where we the readers are intended to be offended by both the unfair distribution as well as harsh consequences. To be clear, even the uneven distribution of the talents strikes us right off the bat as something that an equal opportunity God would not do. The reality is that God does distribute his gifts of intelligence, physical traits, and even drive in a wide spectrum to the human population. Matthew chapter 25 where this parable occurs, is the culmination of a series of offensive chapters that are told in a way as to turn our conventional way of thinking on its head.

The upside down paradoxical way of thinking begins in Matthew chapter 18 when the disciples ask who will be greatest in the kingdom of heaven. The reply by Jesus is that it takes someone humbling themselves like a little child. Next Jesus tells the story of the lost sheep. In that story, the shepherd leaves the 99 to rescue the lost one. This was to be sure an extreme situation even for the shepherds who valued every sheep. We then have the 70 times 7 response as to how often one should forgive their brother. The meaning of this is basically infinity. This appeal for eternal forgiveness is followed by the disturbing story of one who is forgiven a debt but cannot forgive others. With that inability to forgive comes eternal suffering as though that is what happens to us when we cannot forgive life's day to day little offenses repeatedly. The type of thing that begins with "you always...."

Chapter 19 begins with Jesus refuting the legalistic interpretation of divorce. This is followed by the rich young man who wants to know how to get to heaven. Jesus actually gives him 2 ways. The first way to enter life is to keep all the commandments. When the young man replies basically that he has kept the letter of the law, Jesus then challenges him as to the spirit of the law. In that particular situation, the man needed to give all that he owned to the poor and then follow Jesus.

Chapter 20 begins with the parable of the vineyard worker. Here we are offended because those who worked a short amount were paid the same as all day workers. This again troubles us sorely due to inequality of time spent on the project. This parable closes with the rejoinder that some who are first will be last and some that are last will be first. This is followed by the request through a mother, no less, that her sons have a special place in the kingdom, as though they understood the vineyard parable to be about the coming kingdom. Besides the literal challenge to that way of thinking, there is no accident that the only miracle that occurs in this whole stretch is the healing of 2 blind men. They are indeed healed simply because they asked as though we could be too if we only first recognized that we are blind.

Chapter 21 begins with a triumphant entry by Jesus into Jerusalem whereupon he proceeds to literally overturn the temple. Up to this point the figurative way of overturning the traditional way of thinking was all that we had seen. It is as though Jesus is saying that ultimately you must put into action whatever philosophy you espouse. This will be culminated in Matthew chapter 25 at the conclusion of this long sequence. When the Jewish leaders question where Jesus got his authority, Jesus responds with a question about the authority of John the Baptist, knowing that he has them in a quandary because of the latter's popularity.

This is followed by a brief parable about the 2 sons who were asked to do a task. The first one said sure but then didn't get the job done. The second said no but subsequently performed the task. Jesus then spells out that the most despised people of society such as prostitutes and tax collectors will enter heaven before the religious authorities. The parable of the tenants follows to make it clear that they are rejecting Jesus.

Chapter 22 continues this theme of rejection with the parable of the wedding feast. The invitation was broad but few responded. Then it was time for another challenge from the Pharisees to Jesus about paying taxes. The succinct answer by Jesus serves as a perpetual model that everything has its domain. This domain process is further tried regarding the afterlife by the Pharisees. Jesus again has the answer that God is the God of the living and not the dead. This is followed purposely by the greatest commandment of loving God. It is closely followed by the second commandment to love your neighbor as yourself. After some interlude, Jesus will indeed point out later that our neighbor may be who we least expect in Matthew chapter 25.

Chapters 23 and 24 are about the signs of the end and the consequences of not believing.

We return to parables in chapter 25 beginning with the parable of the 10 virgins. This simple parable brings together the virtues of being dedicated, being prepared, and being steadfast. Jesus could have stopped there and we would have got it. Or thought we did. But he had to go and tell the parable of the talents which begins with the first offense of unequal distribution of talents. Next we are offended much like our earlier parable when the 2 investors of success are given the exact same reward despite very different yields on investment. Then we are hit with the biggest challenge of the poor man who actually knew the nature of his master and actually thought he was doing his will by burying the treasure and not taking any chances unlike the other 2. He has harsh consequences. But Jesus does not wish that to be a stand alone concept.

No, this whole long sequence ends with the story of the sheep and goats. Not so much a parable this time as to rather a harsh illustration of what happens if, in the words of Mother Theresa, that we don't recognize Jesus in all of his humble disguises. I was hungry and you fed me. I was thirsty and you gave me drink. I was a stranger and you took me in. I was naked and you clothed me. I was sick and you took care of me. I was in prison and to visited me. All of this is done without judgement and means testing. It is the culmination of this long stretch of offensive stories and actions. It is the heart of the gospel.

Parable of the Talents

The Parable of the Talents is one of those offensive parables that strikes our sensibilities. It begins with an unfair advantage and ends with harsh reality that exacerbates the unequal distribution of talent. We must wonder how anything could be more unchristian if we are being honest. But like all great parables we must get past the surface and expose ourselves to a deeper meaning after we have acknowledged our bias.

The reality is that we do not all come into this world with the same abilities. Sometimes they are even quite disproportionate. We are, it appears, all expected to grow with whatever talents we possess and to not make excuses for what little we perceive. In order to grow we need to take risks. Indeed the Master in the parable seems to not only expect risk taking but to celebrate it as well. Paul Tillich captures this sentiment in his essay "Be not Conformed":

"He who risks and fails can be forgiven. He who never risks and never fails is a failure in his whole being. He is not forgiven because he does not feel he needs forgiveness"

The man with one talent lived simultaneously in the fear of the past of a memory that could not let go of some negativity and at the same time a fear of the future when that exacting demand might happen again. He did not understand the NOW moment. He did not appreciate the complete spectrum of expression of human potential in that he knew only the harsh side of his master but not the loving side. He had perceived the discipline but not felt the love. In so doing he limited himself as well as his opportunity to appreciate the Master.

The other gentlemen worked in the NOW moment. This is not a static moment but one of perpetual growth. It requires awareness of the past, present, and future. It engages life to get the most out of life simply knowing that life requires this of everyone. What they accomplished in material gain was quite small as noted by the Master: you have been faithful over little. Ah yes, but because they exhibit the philosophy of growth, they will be set over much. This the true "Matthew effect". When the Master invites these two to enter into the Joy of the Master, it would appear that they were in a sense already partly there having the satisfaction that they have achieved some reasonable growth. The implication is that by embracing a perspective of perpetual growth that they will now grow beyond their own limits.

Parable of the Vineyard

Perhaps one of the most disturbing parables from the Western mind perspective is the parable of the Workers in the Vineyard found in Matthew chapter 20. We are offended because workers who are hired at the last hour to work in the vineyard are paid the same amount as those hired in the first hour. We displace our disturbance by rationalizing that this is ultimately about salvation and that we wish to welcome even last minute criminals to the Kingdom of heaven. Consider the thief on the cross. Nonetheless, if we are honest, we are offended because the work ethic of many cultures would be that we are mostly rewarded according to our efforts. We do not wish to believe that this could ever remotely apply to someone like Hitler.

First let's review the concept of fairness that Jesus purposely built into the story in order to tap into a belief system that he knew was existent but had limitations. Remember the logistics of this story. Jesus begins by saying that this is a parable about the kingdom of heaven. The owner of a vineyard needs workers to do his work. So he goes and hires local workers to help with the harvest. Most notably the only people who are promised a wage are the first wave of people who are hired in the first hour.

A few hours later the owner goes to marketplace and saw people standing idle. He hires them only with the promise that they will be given what is right. Our subtle disturbance would not have been lost on the original ears. These people were just standing around. No mention was made of effort. Let's be honest. We don't like that. This formula is repeated throughout the day, up to the 11th hour. Let us point out that this is a long day, at least 12 hours. Therefore the first wave of workers were going to end up working 12 hours compared to 1 hour. Or mathematically 12 times as much as much as those hired in the last hour. We are troubled deeply.

We might try to assuage ourselves by noting that this is after all the prerogative of the owner to do with his money whatever he chooses. That might fit well into our Western mindset about ownership. We might also take some peace of mind that this is how the kingdom of God works in terms of salvation. It's not works oriented. Those comfortable with formulas will note it is meant to represent that if the proper formula is recited, that it is irrelevant at what time in a person's life that they utter the formula. This lines up with what is "right" just like the word used by the owner. Such thinking could ensconce us in our comfort zone thinking anachronistically that we get what that generation so long ago did not comprehend. Those who know or read the rest of the chapter might naturally pair this up with what follows immediately.

This vineyard story is followed by the immediate revelation that Jesus is going to Jerusalem where he will be betrayed, condemned, crucified, and rise again. This story now becomes reminiscent of another parable of the vineyard where various workers are killed that the owner sends until finally they kill the owners own son. Now we are getting closer to a formula and story that we can believe in. It makes a distinction between the religious authorities of that age and believers in Jesus. Now we can rest in peace.

Or can we? What if Jesus was telling the story today? Perhaps we might indulge some liberty and say that the first wave of workers were local workers who belonged to the union and were simply laid off. Then we might have various gradations that we would identify less and less with. Let's make the last group illegal aliens who were seasonal migrant workers. Now we are troubled. This isn't fair. That's not the way that the formula works.

But if we continue to extrapolate we might realize that if we are today's religious authorities, that we are troubled when new symbols challenge our representation of God. We fail to appreciate that part of the message is that the God of the Eternal is not bound by a human timeline. Nor is such a God constricted by a formula or a symbol. Jesus pairs this story with his own impending death to remind us that as he has said earlier, that unless a grain falls in to the earth and dies, it cannot bear fruit. But if it dies to self and the notion that it alone has the all time representation of life, truth, and the Eternal- then it can bear fruit.

Vineyard Fairness

Almost as if on cue the disciples had to test the even balance nature of the Parable of the Vineyard by seeing if they could be favored in the kingdom of heaven. Jesus has the end of the parable reflect on the notion that some are upset because the owner has chosen to pay the end of the day workers the same as the beginning of the day workers. The owner reminds the first wave of workers that they got what they were promised and then asks them if they begrudge his generosity. Finally he asks if the disgruntled first wave of workers are envious because the owner is generous.

So enter the disciples James and John with their mother who has come to ask for special privilege in the kingdom of heaven. When Jesus addresses the mother, he seems to do so with more compassion than he does his own mother at the wedding where he performed his first miracle. Given that Jesus performed the request at the first request by his mother after he challenged her approach, it seems only reasonable that he would respond favorably to this request. Not so.

We know at some level that these disciples didn't get the meaning of the moment. But for that matter, it appears that the other disciples did not get it either, because a few moments later they are upset with James and John.

Why would they be upset? Of course, it's possible that all of the disciples still missed the brief interlude in versus 18-20 of Matthew chapter 20 that is sandwiched in between the parable of the vineyard and the family request for privilege. There Jesus spells out the shameful end in which he will be condemned to death, mocked, crucified, and then rise again. The disciples have not grasped the reality here. Maybe they are so used to Jesus speaking in parables that they cannot distinguish the tragic reality here. They appear to be still hoping for a kingdom on earth.

Jesus then gets to some of the heart of the chapter. While the disciples are still struggling with competition for position in however they understand the kingdom, Jesus spells out for them that whoever would be great among them needs to be a servant. But if they want to be first, then according to most versions, they actually need to be the slave. He points out that his own servitude involves the ultimate sacrifice of death.

Then too, we have to have the ironic wrap up to this chapter where the blind men are healed. It is only the blind in this chapter who at the end of a synopsis of the gospel get what Jesus is about. Truly only those who are blind to their preconceptions of truth can have their eyes opened to the ultimate truth.

Shrewd Manager

The parable of the shrewd manager found in Luke chapter 16 is one of those puzzling paradoxes and potentially offensive passages in the gospel. Some of the offense to be clear is subtle. For example in the first sentence we are told about the shrewd manager who was accused of wasting his Masters possessions. We are never told that there's actually truth to that and nor does he even get a trial. Rather the master responds to the hearsay by demanding an account but also pointing out that the manager can no longer be responsible for his possessions. The manager then reviews quickly his options and recognizes that he is losing his job. He recognizes also that he is not capable of doing some other measures such as digging or begging or in other words tasks that involve physical strength or humility for survival. He then crafts a plan that he knows will win him favor when he loses his job.

He does size up that his best option is to actually go to the master's debtors and reduce the amount of debt that each one owes the master.

The shrewd manager even says to at least one of the debtors to make the adjustment quickly as though to not denote so much the urgency but the deviancy. So what does the master do when he finds out about this plot which appears to be rather quickly in the storyline? He actually commends the steward at that point. It is at that time we seemed to have moved from the actual accusation and assumption of being dishonest to owning the title of dishonest.

Here is where the storyline becomes a little more difficult to follow. First of all we must remember that in many parables including the parable of the talents, along with others, the master represents either God or Christ. That may not be the case in this particular parable as we read in verse eight of chapter 16 "for the people of this world are more shrewd in dealing with their own kind then are the people of the light".

By inference this could well strongly imply that the master himself was dishonest. He may well have known all along that the steward was dishonest and overcharged others. He may only have become concerned when he realized that he was not getting his own share. The master may have further realized that he was not going to collect anything on his debtors bills unless the unaffordable was reduced. Jesus next remark is another editorial which advises us to use the worldly wealth to gain friends so that when it is gone we will be welcomed into the eternal dwellings.

This is not to imply that it is a backup plan but rather one of temporality. The statement does indeed recognize the transient nature of the world's goods. Even so Jesus makes it clear that we have a duty of responsibility of stewardship with our earthly possessions. Furthermore, if we are not responsible with other people's possessions we will not be responsible with our own.

So now we have the complete syllogism. First we begin with being responsible with other people's property. This is the same as responsibility with our own property. This in turn shows responsibility with the property of the kingdom of heaven. Put in other terms, all of these values are the same. Ultimately we respect other people's property as our own as well as of the kingdom of heaven. However in order to show that we are not to get hung up on either positions or money, Jesus reminds us that we cannot serve two masters. One master may well be money, the other one literally God. We are reminded elsewhere that he said where your treasure is there will your heart be also. We might flip that around and say where our heart is, there will be our treasure. Our intentions must be reflected both in our attitude as well as in our actions.

Family Offense

Jesus spares no offense when he takes on the hallowed ground of family. In Matthew chapter 10 he is quite clear that he has come to turn son against father, daughter against mother, etc but also that someone's usual enemies will be part of his household. While this all seems to be part of the harsh support that he gives the disciples when they go on their mission work, it is to send a message that the commitment to truth has a high cost.

A few chapters later he will have a very clear demonstration of that principle. In chapter 13 Jesus' mother and brothers show up wanting to speak to him. He asks the rhetorical question of who is his mother and brothers and then proceeds to point out that it is anyone who does the will of his father in heaven. All of this is indeed offensive to us and there is no easy way to soften the blow if we literalize here. But if we substitute Jesus own words that he is the Way, Truth, and the Light, we might be able to apply a word like Truth here and go on the offensive by making it actionable to stick up for truth and to promote truth wherever it is applicable.

This segment in Matthew is followed by the Parable of the Sower. This is the parable told right after the disciples foray into the mission fields. The message here is that they are not responsible for what the seed bears, only for the sowing. They are responsible for disseminating the truth in all of its forms by realizing that truth has a higher value than family or religious tradition. It is not inherently antithetical to the institutions. Rather, it is just that it supersedes them. We must keep in mind that we are not to get lost along the way as can happen in any religious fold. This is of course the meaning of the Good Samaritan in which religious leaders on their way to perpetuate the knowledge of the law failed to grasp his application. All of this once again culminates in the Judgment day parable told in Matthew 25 about how the righteous are saved by virtue of their unwitting actions of helping those in need.

Rich Fool Part 1

Who is the Parable of the Rich Fool written for? The prelude is someone who appears to be denied an inheritance and wants Jesus to send a message of correction. First it is easy to interpret the parable as written about and against anybody who is rich. It is convenient. We could also take it as Jesus warning the man who asked the question.

Arguably Jesus does answer the man's question with a warning to the brother who is not sharing. After all, is this not the meaning of greed in that one tries to retain too much for oneself. The parable in all versions notes the man talking to himself as self in the egoic sense. The Message by Eugene Petersen captures this well at the conclusion. "that's what happens when you fill your barns with self and not with God".

The perceptive individual realizes of course that the parable was given for themselves. But what if there was another meaning that went beyond the obvious. The rich man does not appear to be in trouble until he asks what is he going to do with all his wealth. We are given the impression that he already has enough and now is going to store more for himself. Notably he is not showing signs of sharing this vast wealth that appears to have materialized by nature's hand and not his own.

Perhaps Jesus is answering the man's question after all. Or perhaps there is even more. What if another meaning was that the man was not condemned except by his own hand and only when he stopped growing. Read it again. Is this interpretation not possible? Put another way he was not blessed by his own hand but when he took credit, kept it for himself, and then stopped growing, that was when he felt the hand of self condemnation.

The parable is not simply one of greed. It is that we are blessed with measures for which we did very little. When we do not recognize that and furthermore do not make our own subsequent efforts to continue the growth process, then again we are self condemned. This parable is about recognition. The man does not recognize that he has enough. But how does anyone know when they have enough? When they give some away. What we have is not our own, but when we attempt to keep it for self, those possessions then come to own us.

The Rich Man, Creation, and The Ego

The setup in Luke chapter 12 for the key parable seems to provide little doubt at first glance who the intended audience was. Given that the chapter starts with a warning about the religious leaders and the potential need to be on guard around their teachings, it would seem that the parable was at some level intended for them. Of course, it may be for the brother who would not share, or even the man himself who asked Jesus to make the brother share.

Surely the parable is for most rich people or at least the greedy. Of course, we must always see ourselves written into the parables if we are going to have full application. Like any good parable the rich fool was written for multiple parties. Yet there are multiple meanings that are easily overlooked when we fixate on one meaning, especially one that is applicable to those including ourselves. Perhaps we need to look at the first chapter in the Bible all the way back to Genesis.

There we have the original creation story as it occurs in the Original Testament. God the creator is creating all kinds of living organisms ultimately as a reflection of a collective being. This creative origin comes out in the culmination of creating humankind. In Genesis 1:26 we read in the NIV the words let us create humankind in our image. Who are the other parts of "the our and us"? Many have used this as a convenient theological reference to our modern trinity with Jesus Christ and the Holy Spirit.

The problem with that thinking is that it simply cannot be extracted from Genesis. Rather the closest description we have of "our" image is what immediately follows. God created humankind in the image of God, male and female. This potentially implies that God has both feminine and masculine traits. We will not go into depth here on the implications of this feminine side of God. To us Genesis seems to make this source of an inclusive God as a given.

The stewardship is where we wish to focus first. It would appear to us that in the creation story humans are given stewardship in which there is a management role but not one of classic dominion. Our goal as avowed meat eaters is not to make the Genesis story as a case for vegetarianism, except that those who do so could argue a long way. Humankind is given only seed-bearing plants to eat and fruit with seeds. No animals. The animals are given by God green plants. It would appear then that our role as stewards for the animals is to protect their food sources since they may not always be able to.

So, it appears that we have a unified creation where everything both has its place and support system. All is well until a choice by the ego is made to be more like the image of God as the ego perceives God. Humans have not realized that they are at the time of creation basically one with all of creation including God. They desire to be distinct and thus above the God of unity. At some time, a creature known as the serpent is introduced, but to be clear the appeal is to the humans first creation-the ego.

We believe that it is only in this context that we can fully understand the parable of the rich man in Luke chapter 12. Yes, this parable has a point to those who would set themselves up to act separately or in the place of God, be they religious leaders or otherwise. Such are separatists and not upholding the stewardship of creation. Jesus goes on to warn about all kinds of greed as though there are many types which may not be so obvious. All of them involve the ego trying to be separate.

Let's examine the parable closely. The story begins with the rich man not necessarily doing anything to obtain his riches. Rather we are told that the ground produced a great yield. Understandably he wishes to build a bigger storehouse. This is not what he appears condemned for. He is not condemned until he announces that he will not work for many years but will rather take it easy. The fact that he will eat, drink, and be merry does not appear to be the cause of his condemnation.

Rather the condemnation appears to come when he sets himself apart from God and the creation. This is the work of the ego. The ego steps out of its role in a unified creation and wants something for the self. It is seldom grateful, much like our rich man here. It is never satisfied. This appears to be the blasphemy against the unity of the Holy Spirit that is warned about in the prelude to the parable. Separating the self from creation is not unforgivable by God, but the choice to be an eternal separate ego is an eternal condemnation. Indeed an argument an be made that the man has chosen to no longer be the steward of the land as charged in Genesis.

The Unjust Judge

In the parable of the unjust judge Jesus compares his own Heavenly Father to an unjust judge. To do so he tells the story of a widow woman who beseeches the judge day and night for her petition. The unjust judge will have nothing to do with her. But she is persistent. Finally he has had enough. He says rather begrudgingly that although he doesn't care about the woman or her cause that he will grant her the concern in order to get on with his life. The analogy is meant to offend us. To offend us into action and persistence even in the face of unlikely outcomes.

The analogy though may have deeper connection with the prodigal. In this case the Father represents the Just God at the start of the story who becomes the Unjust God upon the return of the prodigal. In so doing he has waived the right for justice in favor of redemption or the imputed righteousness of Christ.

Mountains, Mustard Seeds, and Perverts

To more fully understand and appreciate the statement that Jesus made in Matthew chapter 17 verse 26 we must return to the start of the chapter where we encounter the transfiguration. Like many chapters it is a story of great vicissitudes. We begin the chapter with 3 disciples ascending literally and figuratively great heights as they experience the transfiguration. The strong Jewish connection with Jesus connection with Moses and Elijah is shown in great light by no less than God.

Just as Moses could not look directly at the burning bush, so too the disciples fell to the ground in great fear. Then literally they were touched by Jesus. Following that they saw none of the overwhelming flash of light. Nor did they see Moses or Elijah. Except that perhaps they did and still did not realize it. Indeed in this flashing instance Jesus has fused the great Jewish traditions of Moses and Elijah and God into himself. He will be the light of the world so well depicted in John's gospel.

But do these enlightened disciples really understand? Jesus answers some of their questions explaining the symbolism that he stands for. He talks openly about his death but they seem oblivious. In fact they are fixated on Elijah and the symbolic connection with John the Baptist. This is even after Jesus mentions a second time that he is going to suffer. Their understanding coming down the mountain is not what you would expect for their mountaintop experience.

So if the special experience disciples do not get the connections, what do we expect from the disciples back at ground level? The ground level disciples have been apparently challenged by a boy with seizures that they are unable to heal. Jesus calls them perverse and unbelieving. Later the perverts go to Jesus in private and ask Jesus why they could not heal the child. Jesus points out that it is because they have such little faith.

Paradoxically though, they don't need much faith. All they need is faith like the very tiny mustard seed. This seed has the ability to grow rapidly into a tall plant that was ubiquitous in that region. It may grow up to 10 feet the first year before reaching a final height of up to 25 feet. It needs very little rainfall to sustain itself. When mature it has multiple root systems that add to its strength. These are measures that the disciples would have understood better than the Transfiguration experience.

There are many metaphors that are obvious with the mustard seed. So obvious that we deceive ourselves by thinking that we have the answers that the disciples just did not get because of either lack of faith or ignorance. But there are hidden meanings that escape us such as the mustard seed is simply doing what it was designed to do as a simple tiny seed. Yet it cannot complete its existential purpose without a very interconnected root system that is at the ground level. Get that faith, we are told, and you can do more than have a mountaintop experience. You can move mountains of misunderstandings.

The Prodigal

The prodigal son is often viewed as the culmination of the trio of the lost. The triad begins with a concept familiar to the Jewish people well before King David made his reference to rescuing lost sheep. In this case the shepherd, who may not even be the owner goes out of his way for merely one of his hundred sheep. In the next saga, it is a woman who goes after one of the ten coins that is lost. The epitome of seeking the lost is when one out of two is sought out which is the case of the prodigal. We would do well to not lose sight of the notion that all of these were people of some means who were missing something. With two brief setups Jesus has set the stage to involve unexpected twists by involving women of some means, inanimate objects as well as familiar symbols.

But here's the next big twist in that when a human is involved, the owner not only does not go looking for the lost, but arguably provides the means for him to stay away, provided that he not squander it all. This is the ultimate expression of free will that the Father allows. Unlike the setup stories, the Father stays put with no visible effort for searching. It is almost as though we were told the setups to show not only parallels, but also to dramatize the difference.

Rather, he lets the son initiate the return. He even lets him present his well rehearsed speech of repentance on how he has sinned against heaven, the father, etc. The speech is essential even though it seems to be quickly glossed over by the father who turns the tables and plans a huge welcome. It is almost as though Jesus has done everything he can to be offensive to his audience in this parable.

First, uncharacteristically, the younger brother has asked for his share of the inheritance prematurely. Then after riotous living by the son, the father runs to meet him which is totally out of character for such a Jewish father. We are meant to see this progression of being out of character when he rebukes the faithful older brother and then rewards the wayward son in everyone's presence. We are meant to be offended in order to see our own role in the parable.

We can easily be pulled in too far if we make this a situation of unconditional forgiveness in which the two brothers simply flip flop status. To be clear, this is a father who wishes to be fair and go by the rules. We are mistaken if we think that everything is going to be roses for the Prodigal. He has already received his inheritance and will in all likelihood fall into a role not unlike he mentions in his repentance speech.

This story is indeed about change. One son changes when he sees what is steady and unchangeable in his father. The faithful and pious son does not change, but needs to. He has expectations of a materialistic reward if he remains faithful. The father is indeed unwavering, but has no need to change. He points out that the faithful and pious son has always had access to everything but somehow never recognized it or appreciated it. The pious son did not live in the Now, but was always working for the future which would never exist for him because he could not recognize that it was always there. The Prodigal son lived in the Now both when he squandered his inheritance and when he returned home. This is the Fathers true joy when he recognizes that the prodigal lives in the Now. The father promotes the Now moment further by celebrating the moment but also in recognizing when that moment is over. Listen to the words in the ERV: but this <u>was</u> a day to be happy and celebrate. Or in the Good News Bible: we had to celebrate and be happy because your brother was dead but Now is alive. He was lost but Now he is found. The tenses used imply that the celebrations will be over if they weren't already. But at the same time people are to Be happy. This tense implies a more permanent state of Being.

We are told that the pious son is angry and we are fairly certain why. It seems so obvious that we ourselves are a bit offended and somewhat angry as well at the circumstances. But we don't really want to be angry at the prodigal so we displace our anger to the older pious brother. But the faithful brother is angry about the past of the brother who has squandered money and angry at the future he senses. He senses that the prodigal will be favored unfairly given the lavish welcome. But there is no evidence that such will continue. Rather the prodigal is likely about to begin his servitude.

Indeed this parable is ultimately about slavery. The prodigal is clearly a slave to his passions. He is furthermore willing to work as a hired servant and arguably even a slave upon his return. The discerning individual realizes that he will ultimately be beholden to the older faithful brother upon the death of their father. But the faithful older brother is also a slave even in his own eyes as is captured well in the ERV and other versions: Look for all these years I have worked like a slave for you…..he then goes on to lament how he never had a party, etc. He refers to the prodigal brother to his father as "this son of yours" as though he himself was not a son but rather the slave he referenced earlier. He did not live in the Now, but rather the dead past of his brother's sins or the imagined deficit of his future inheritance. Effectively the younger brother is a willing slave and the older brother an unwilling slave.

The parable and the chapter ends rather abruptly leaving us longing for justice for the older son and a reconciliation. First we desire to see a reconciliation with the father and then later the prodigal. Finally we must not forget that the faithful elder son is estranged from his work. He worked like a slave and felt like one, never enjoying the fruits of his labor. The parable begins with estrangement and ends with estrangement. Abruptly.

Jesus Sweats Blood

The story of Jesus sweating blood as he approaches his arrest and ultimate crucifixion is told only in the Gospel of Luke and the 22nd chapter. Luke was by many accounts the only physician to record the works and the life of Jesus. Perhaps this gives him the unique ability to describe this rare event known medically as hematidrosis. We do need to keep in mind though that Luke presented a simile and that Jesus sweat fell to the ground like blood dripping from an open wound.

The most common explanations given for the simile is that it portends the concern for the extreme physical suffering that will occur shortly to Jesus to the point of crucifixion as an innocent man. Even before the crucifixion there will be great physical torture. Likely he was food and fluid deprived before being flogged substantially even as he was abandoned by those closest to him. While Matthew and Mark do not use the blood simile they do reference that Jesus soul was overwhelmed with sorrow to the point of death.

These graphic descriptions seem to portray Jesus human side in order for us to both relate to his extreme suffering and appreciate what he endured on behalf of the human race. Furthermore this whole event seems to fit a tidy version of the formula that is traced back to the Original Testament in which we are told that without the shedding of blood that there is no forgiveness. While there is indeed a great sacrifice involved here we would do well to examine the context of this significant event.

This is a great existential moment for Jesus that indeed reflects the existential moment that Abraham felt when he climbed the mountain believing that he had to sacrifice his only son that he had waited so long for. On the night in which he was betrayed he prays to God to have this cup of suffering taken from him, but he does not wish to abandon the will of God. At that God sends an angel to strengthen him. This strength allows him to pray more earnestly which then leads to the heavy sweating blood simile.

The reality that is often missed is that Jesus is at the existential moment giving up a significant portion of the power of God. We are, after all, told in his own words that if he appealed to God he would send down a legion of angels to spare him of a painful death. It is interesting that Jesus will not invoke the power that he does ask his only disciples to be prepared with swords. When the disciples before this agony prayer respond to Jesus that they have two swords he tells them that this is enough.

We maintain that the anguish that Jesus experiences in this existential moment is the mental suffering of recognizing that if after all of this preparation with his disciples that they still do not get his mission. Even at the last supper in which he reveals his ultimate fate the disciples are still disputing which one of them will be greatest in the kingdom of heaven. Even when he is in anguish in the garden they have fallen asleep. Nor do they understand the meaning of the swords and their purpose.

It would appear that the great anguish of Jesus is that people neither understand his mission and that he foresees a great misuse of power. In the garden he is literally in no man's land where he does not have the support of his comrades on earth and struggles with whether this is the best way to complete the mission as he understands it and whether or not to invoke a power that is his for the asking.

Stephen Harrison and Richard Huizinga

The Cross as Mystery

If we were to ask is the cross more of a miracle or a mystery we would quickly deduce that it was more of a mystery. To be clear this does not include the resurrection where the debate reaches different proportions. Speaking strictly about the cross however, we could almost say that the cross is anti- miraculous. This is because God does not perform the miracle that we know he could and that Jesus himself references to extricate Jesus from his dilemma. If we are honest with ourselves, we are a little offended that God does not come to the rescue of his only begotten son. The cross therefore represents a suspension of power even of legitimate power. The cross as symbol represents the destruction of power. The cross represents God's desire to challenge our human interpretation of power.

Why are we challenged in all of the synoptic Gospels to take up our cross and follow Jesus? This is of course a metaphor for the believer and not an actual sacrifice in the fleshly sense which only a small percentage of Christians over the course of many centuries have been asked to perform. We are therefore asked to sacrifice and put on hold our own understanding of legitimate power. We are asked to sacrifice our understanding of our own ultimate symbol.

We must keep in mind what we are instructed to do before we take up our cross. We are, according to all three synoptic gospels, to deny ourselves. This is not so much a denial in the physical sense but in the psychological sense of all of the things that we seem so certain of but do not fully grasp. We deny the apparent certainty of the familiar in order to attain the eternal mystery.

In one of his most simplistic parables, Jesus notes that unless a grain of wheat falls to the earth and dies, it bears no fruit. But if it dies, it can bear much fruit. Our symbols of ourselves as well as even our ultimate symbols need to die in order to bear the fruit that they are capable of bearing.

Mystery in the New Testament

For this topic we wish to distinguish mystery from miraculous. Miraculous is something applied to an event that must by nature be on the order of a miracle, or a temporary suspension of nature by the supernatural. We might open up the New Testament and note that right off the bat that Jesus birth is considered a miracle since he is born to a virgin. Well and good.

But the birth of a baby who has a divine mission to fulfill is a mystery. Why didn't God come as fully developed human as opposed to an infant? For that matter, why come at all. Jesus himself said that people had Moses and the prophets and did not believe them. That itself is a mystery. We don't need a miracle to trump a mystery. The rule of mystery is that when one mystery disappears, another mystery appears. Miracles attempting to trump miracles is Original Testament like Moses versus the magicians of Pharaoh.

Mystery replacing mystery is New Testament. Jesus being led by the Spirit into the wilderness is mystery. Jesus being tempted by Satan is mystery. This is apparently what a major religious leader struggled with in the Lord's Prayer recently, and had language adjusted to fit the modern era. Lead us not into temptation becomes "keep us from the evil one". Apparently we are above Jesus the Christ in that he can be delivered to the Evil One, whereas we are above such musings.

God choosing parable and paradox to convey Truth is mystery beyond miracle. God chooses to bypass miracles on behalf of his own Son at his hours of biggest challenge. The first time is when Jesus has been in the wilderness and then meets up with Satan who proceeds to try to engage Jesus in a show to display miraculous intervention to rescue Jesus. Also, we have the cross where Jesus resists the human urge to have God put on a power surge and take over the destructive proceedings. This is mystery superseding miraculous.

Well and good again. But what about the resurrection? Isn't that proof that the miraculous supersedes the mysterious? The mystery remains as to why someone who had the opportunity to sit at the right hand of God for eternity would choose to have any remaining time on earth given the tremendous and ultimate sacrifice that they had already made. The mystery remains when we are told by the Master himself that we will do greater things than him. Is that because we will have incredible miraculous powers or because we will see beyond the miraculous to engage people in the Mystery of Life coupled with the paradox that in order for something to bear fruit that it must first die?

Temptation

CHAPTER 4

Temptation like Jesus

It sounds strange, but if we want to be like Jesus, then we need to be tempted. At some level we even want to be tempted. Before Jesus could begin his mission, he needed to be tempted. What was that for? Who was that for? Some will point out that it was to show his power over Satan. Really? Does a believer with a modicum of faith, let's say even with less than a grain of mustard, have any doubt about that power. Surely we don't think that Jesus himself needed to have a stronger conviction. We also find the notion that such temptation experience was a model for us on how to deal with and overcome temptation a bit disingenuous. After all, aren't all stories on Jesus of this nature of modeling? Was this intersection of human challenge and divine response an opportunity for us moderns to relook at the perspective for today?

Jesus submits willingly to the temptation after the peak of baptism. At the moment when he appears to be filled with as clear of endorsement of the mission of God that anyone could have. Indeed the gospel of Mark captures this succinctly. Immediately Jesus is sent into the wilderness for temptation by no less than the Spirit. How do we contrast that with the haunting phrase in the Lord's Prayer, "lead us not into temptation"?

Is that something God does for a hobby when bored? Are we actually saying God please don't be tempted to tempt us? Are we saying "look God, we know if your own son can be led by the Spirit into the throws of temptation, then there is a fairly good chance that we might as well". So could you avoid that? Please?

What about in the garden when Jesus is in agony, feeling abandoned, feeling betrayed about his imminent death? Why does he pray that if it is possible that this cup pass? Is that some remnant of temptation? Is that the fulfillment of the wilderness experience where we are told after the successful refutation of Jesus, that Satan departed until an opportune time? In the first temptation setting in Mark Jesus demonstrates the ability to live with the natural fears of the wild and unknown as we have elaborated on elsewhere. The latter account in the garden is not, as is often portrayed, a projection of our human fears, but rather a reflection of healthy human doubt.

Jesus himself is questioning the way to fulfill the mission of God. Before he sacrifices his life he is willing to sacrifice his own understanding of a divine mission. So too when we think we have captured the essence of God's work, would we do well to pray and even sweat blood to see if we should sacrifice our own interpretation of God's will for the actual one?

Going Deeper into Temptation

If we are honest the Temptations of Jesus trouble us on several levels. If Jesus is part of the Godhead then how is it possible for him even to be tempted? Next, if the Spirit is part of the Godhead, how is it that in all three synoptic Gospels Matthew, Mark, and Luke that mentioned the temptation, that Jesus was led by the spirit into the wilderness to be tempted? If we wish to identify that Jesus was both man and God and by virtue of his being a man needed to be tempted, then how do we reconcile that it was the spirit who led him into the arena of temptation? Are we to believe that it is the spirit that participates in our own temptations?

Next without getting bogged down in a protracted discussion of how and why different gospels present different accounts of stories, suffice it to say that the only common ground of the three gospel stories of temptation is that both the spirit and the devil are involved.

The Gospel of Mark mentions no specific temptation but implies that Jesus may well have been tempted for 40 days by the devil. Both the Gospels of Matthew and Luke have the temptations occurring after 40 days of fasting. Matthew and Luke include the first temptation after fasting as to secure food. This is rebuffed by Jesus with the statement that man should not live by bread alone.

They both include the temptation to fame and power if Jesus will worship Satan. Jesus reply is again straight forward in that we are to worship only God. Echoes of this experience are seen in the Lord's Prayer in Matthew chapter 6. Here Jesus begins the prayer so often recited with "Our Father". We have discussions elsewhere on this whole prayer, but our purpose here is to make the connection with the wilderness experience. The model prayer puts an emphasis on worshiping God as Jesus did in the wilderness. Immediately following this statement is the request or even the demand for God to give us our daily bread. Is this spiritual bread or the physical type? After we tell God to make sure he forgives our sins, we are then to tell him not to lead us into temptation. Is that something God or the Spirit of God is prone to?

We may debate the actual meaning of these phrases but at some level they are offensive to our sensibilities. They are not, we submit, ultimately there for a catchy memorable worship formula. They are there to highlight the most actionable measure of the prayer, namely that we are to forgive in order to have the spirit of forgiveness in our own life.

Stephen Harrison and Richard Huizinga

Temptation Revisited

Once again if we are honest we have to admit that we are bothered by the temptation presentation in Matthew and Luke. We like the idea that he was tempted because that made him more human. It made him more like us. It showed that we can be powerful and resist temptation even when we are deprived of basic needs or offered the world. But we are still offended because we want to see a little more of a power play against the devil. We want something a little more dramatic. We certainly don't want the door left open for a future temptation as Luke very much notes that the devil departed for an opportune time.

Opportune time? That is every day for the rest of us.

We might benefit from less drama, as is found in the oldest gospel of Mark. There we have the more realistic approach implying that Jesus was tempted all along by Satan in his wilderness experience. No drama of leaping off tall buildings. No extremes of worshiping Satan to get the whole world's kingdoms. Probably more practical stuff like getting Jesus to second guess his mission. Maybe some stuff like Look, God already said after your baptism that he was well pleased with you and that he loved you. You don't have to do anything more. Plus why risk what you are doing when you might mess up.

We feel that the other authors tried to capture the sensation of this temptation about being comfortable about fulfilling the mission of God and accordingly felt they had to dramatize it as something of a power play. Most of us can resist that type of temptation. We probably won't challenge the laws of gravity after any period of time, even with food deprivation. Believing in a higher permanent reward is more than enough to have us resist directly worshipping Satan. Also, 40 days or so without food is not a lot different time span than 40 days plus a few verses, or few minutes, or even few hours of temptations. Mark also notes that he was this entire time with the wild animals.

That's perhaps where the temptations were. Jesus had to master the fear that is in every human being. This is what the wild animals meant. The subtlety of the devil is that he identifies our fears and works to capitalize on them. He wants us to rationalize that God would want us to have basic things like food and water. He wants us further to be comfortable in the accomplishments that we have already achieved for the kingdom so that we will not do more. He wants us reveling in the cloud of glory after our baptism with the very real feeling that God loves us and is well pleased with us. That is the most opportune time, when we feel that we have captured God's love and that he is pleased without us doing anything more. As well intentioned that Matthew and Luke may have been in their elaborations, we must not miss the opportune time of rationalization and complacency. We need to move on as Jesus did with a brief time with the angels after every temptation and get on with the difficulties of working with imperfect people as was the next move of Jesus.

The mission

Satan gives Jesus an opportunity to define his mission. We conveniently forget the role that temptation provides which is to define what we are and what we are not. We must embrace temptation to define ourselves.

1. In refusing to convert the stones into bread Jesus resists the self serving urge to satisfy a natural hunger with something unnatural.

2. After refusing the opportunity to be in charge of all that is visible, Jesus chooses rather to take charge of that which is invisible– The inner self.
3. In refusing to put himself in harm's way, he anticipates everyone who wishes to abdicate responsibility for their own well-being and appeal for rescue miracle.

Jesus then goes on in Luke chapter 4 to give a more positive image of what his mission is. That mission is to preach to the poor who are the people unseen in the margins. It is also to give sight to the people who are literally blind – which is perhaps easier than giving insight to those with preconceptions.

After Jesus reads a prophecy, he notes that today that prophecy is fulfilled. Specifically is fulfilled in the now, doing something, and not some future oriented time. This disturbs the status quo and threatens to unbalance the power which allows oppression. Jesus mission is to allow people to see things differently than they have seen before.

The Not So Unreasonable Temptations of Jesus

One must keep in mind that Jesus temptations are not entirely unreasonable ones even for people of stature to encounter. Having one's daily needs including eating and appropriate recognition are reasonable things to consider. However it is clear that Jesus senses it is a higher goal and higher calling in Luke 4:18. In this sequence which follows the actual temptations of Jesus we see that Jesus senses his own mission as something above and beyond what Satan was offering him. Quite clearly Jesus senses his mission as reaching out to those who otherwise have not been reached. This includes the prisoners and the blind and all who are oppressed.

Jesus then goes on to point out to his hometown area that that mission has been fulfilled. The towns people express what so many of us sense in our own lives, namely that while there are answers right in front of us, we are blind to them. To carry the analogy that has been set up, we are blind to her own opportunities and we are oppressed and poor because of refusing to recognize what we have in front of us. Sometimes it takes a truly deprived individual to appreciate the blessings and opportunities that are available to them.

Struggling With Temptation

Only he who confronts that what he struggles or wrestles with can grow beyond himself or out of himself. This is the story of Jacob in the Original Testament. It is echoed also by Emerson's statement that no one understands a truth until he contends with it:

> Only he who is tempted can relate. Because Jesus was tempted he is able to define the true self and overcome barriers that allow him to help others.

All decisions are ultimately temptations.

Therefore we all wish to be tempted. Because we all desire that existentialist decision. In fact as the existentialists have noted, a decision is the only thing that is required.

A decision means a choice. We must choose between two measures: will I or will I not. This implies looking at the past and reviewing the pleasure/pain and the risk/reward equation as well as anticipating the future.

Therefore the decision is that timeless moment which incorporates the past and the present and the future at the apex of the decision point.

A child does not see this past or present tense. A teenager sees the past but not much of the future. Yet we envy both because each possesses some of the Now moment while we strive for the enlightened awareness of the past and future. We would not sacrifice that awareness, but we would love that spontaneity– And so we enter into temptation.

We do not wish to have the truth of God lead us into a temptation much as the Lord's prayer implores us. We might pause to ask why do we tell God to not do something that seems rather like he would not do. But, **we** lead ourselves to the precipice of temptation much as Jesus was led to the precipice to experience his own temptation. Furthermore we wish to have the internal synthesizer that sometimes passes for God to lead us to that moment where we can sense the freedom sometimes known as spontaneity and have conscious awareness give us a reconciliation of the timeless glimpse. So yes we seek temptation.

What about the "WOE!" factor. After all another Scripture tells us that woe to him by whom temptations come. This statement seems to presume a warning built in or a punishment. Once again consider flipping this around and saying that perhaps the WOE factor refers to an individual dying to self that would never happen unless temptations come. We are assured that temptations are to come though.

We might ask ourselves therefore, is there an opportune time for temptations to arise. Actually the Scriptures give us that answer in Jesus own temptations. When Jesus' own temptations were completed we are told that Satan departed for an opportune time. We are led to believe that that opportune time refers to Satan's own timetable. However what if that opportune time for temptation referred to the individual and not the devil. Perhaps an opportune time referred to Jesus own timing as opposed to some force of evil.

Let's walk through the temptations that Jesus experienced. In the first temptation to turn stone into bread, Jesus replies that man should not live by bread alone. To us it would appear that Jesus is actually resisting the temptation to change something from its natural state that is a stone to something that we eat. Just because we are hungry does not seem to be liberty or license to change something from its natural state to another state. The reader can make his own implications about food additives. We need to keep in mind that in the Lord's Prayer Jesus tells us that we are to give a command to God that we receive our daily bread. That is we are to demand not simply ask. Elsewhere we hear echoes of Jesus temptation summarized in the scripture when Jesus reminds us that which of us as parents would give our children a stone if they asked for Bread. This practical advice has some deep significance in Jesus own life.

The next temptation regarding jumping off the cliff is another reminder that we are not to request to do something unnatural. We don't need to set up an artificial temptations to push the limits of the natural. More bluntly we're not to expose ourselves to physical harm and expect great results.

In the third and final temptation Jesus is asked to worship the visible as opposed to the invisible. Jesus is sending a subtle message that reminds us that we are to worship what we do not know but that does know us and that knows our needs before you ask him. Once again we get to tell God our natural needs and expect them to be honored

When we are presented with choices it means that we must weigh in on the outcomes just as Jesus in these three temptations. Keep in mind he neither asked for or received divine intervention. In fact it is helpful to realize that the angels come only after Jesus has dealt with Satan and is done with Satan. Also there is a subtle implication that Jesus has acquired skills that he developed by the temptation and not by supernatural intervention later in the chapter. There is the scene where when he is confronted with an angry mob that he simply walked through their midst. This is thus a skill that he would not have developed without that inner discipline that comes from being able to encounter temptation and therefore make a decision.

When Peter Tempted Jesus

We tend to think of temptations as coming only from Satan. We generally don't think of them as coming from our close associates or friends. That, however, is exactly what happened to Jesus. Who was that associate and comrade? No less than Simon Peter. The story may be found in Mark chapter 8 and Matthew chapter 16. The setting in both is that Jesus has just fed several thousand people with a few small loaves. The next thing we have some religious leaders coming to him and demanding a sign or miracle. Apparently they got wind of the feeding and wanted to know for themselves. The Good News Bible notes that Jesus groaned over the question. Jesus will not appease them with a miracle. A miracle comes at a practical time of need, not by request for unbelievers.

Jesus will then heal a blind man, though interestingly, the first attempt did not produce clear sight. Was that weakness of faith on the blind man or was it to show the challenges of healing for even a master healer? The first attempt Jesus leads him by the hand out of the village and spits on his eyes. Jesus appears to not know if the technique will be successful. He asks him if he can see anything. When the blind man replies that he sees men that look like trees, Jesus tries again. What a story. Jesus doesn't know what we can see until we tell him. We maintain that there is another analogy in this story that will unfold momentarily.

So now we have 2 miracles performed and Jesus telling both his own disciples as well as the religious leaders that they are missing the boat. So he asks them who people say he is. The reports say famous prophets like Elijah while others say even John the Baptist. Jesus wants to know specifically who the disciples say he is. Peter proceeds to make his bold profession that Jesus is the Messiah. Jesus warns the disciples to tell no one. Jesus next points out that his mission involves death and resurrection. At that moment the same Peter who just made his profession took Jesus aside to rebuke him. Immediately Jesus turns and sees the other disciples and says to Peter to "Get thee behind me Satan".

Jesus is accusing Peter of having only human concerns in mind. Peter is only seeing part of the mission of Jesus. He sees only the miracles. Accordingly, he is like the blind man who was partially healed. He can only see the part of the mission that he wants to. He is not only blind to the suffering, but he does not realize that he is tempting Jesus to ignore the essential suffering and symbolic sacrifice. That is why Jesus has to use the strong language of Satan getting behind him. Earlier Jesus quoted

Original Testament scripture to Satan to not put the Lord your God to the test. Effectively that is what Jesus is saying to Peter. Yes God can be tempted or at least put to the test by anyone who thinks they understand a part of his mission but doesn't get the sacrifice part.

Little Children

Matthew chapter 18 gives a seemingly strong endorsement and support for little children. Jesus states very clearly that unless we change and become like little children, that we will never enter the kingdom of heaven. Never enter. Pretty strong language. What did he really mean? What does a child represent?

Children are naive on the one hand but also not addicted to a particular way of thinking. Children bring a freshness along with acceptance. They tend to be inclusive unless they have been caused to sin by the introduction of prejudice. Remember what triggered Jesus initial remarks on this topic was the question by Jesus own disciples as to who is the greatest in the kingdom of heaven. His challenge answer is to be like little children. Not to be little children. Like little children. Unpretentious.

We are told that anyone who causes someone like a child to sin will have severe consequences. Don't lose sight of the analogy. The children are metaphors for those who have not been led astray by the system. They may believe something merely because it is told though they are sponges for absorbing stories. Because they do believe what they are told, the more mature believers must be cautious about introducing beliefs that don't contribute to the Ultimate Truth. They must be careful about getting the newcomers hooked on creeds that mistake the symbol for that Ultimate Truth. We are being told basically not to tempt them into the sense of wanting to belong like children do, by forcing our interpretations of symbols on them. Basically we are being told not to tempt them and cause them to fall away from that Truth. Jesus knew that little children do already have a hierarchy from an early age that they follow. They do indeed have an idea of who the biggest is, who the best is, who the leader is etc. We must not confuse their innocence with total unawareness. By the same token we would do well to not confuse Jesus symbolic use of children with the metaphor that they were intended for. Basically we are being strongly warned to not cause new believers who want to be part of the fold to mistake our interpretation of the Truth for the Ultimate Truth.

Tempting Jesus From Satan to His Best Friend and Beyond

Elsewhere we have discussed the temptation of Jesus and then later how his lead disciple Peter tempted him shortly after Peter makes the great profession that Jesus is the Messiah. When you are the king of anything, everyone wants to challenge you and take you on in some way. If, after all, your best friend and lead disciple can tempt you, then why not those somewhat between him and Satan. Enter the religious leaders of Jesus day. For our purposes here we will include putting God to the test as somewhat analogous to temptation at some level. We examine three stories to explore this testing experience.

The first test we reference here is the story found in John chapter 8. There we see the religious leaders bringing to Jesus a woman who was caught in the act of adultery. We can't really know what the motive behind those religious leaders was. Ostensibly it was to see if Jesus would honor the laws of Moses and agree that due to her sin that she should be stoned to death. Jesus is initially silent though he does write something that remains a mystery in the sand. We have expounded on this elsewhere. When he speaks it is with a penetrating voice to their conscience. He does not refute the law of Moses. He merely goes to the heart of the meaning.

For our next story we turn to Matthew chapter 22. Jesus has delivered a series of parables that cut to the heart of those who reject the freshness and joy of God's message including the parable of the tenants as well as the parable of the wedding banquet. We pick the story up in verse 15 of Matthew chapter 22 where we are told that religious leaders developed a plan to trap Jesus in his own words. In a way that is not fully appreciated by everyone, some of our biggest tests come when strong words of truth are applied in inappropriate ways. They call Jesus Teacher and a man of integrity who teaches the way of God according to the truth without paying attention to the words or status of others. After that crafty setup, they then ask if it is right to pay taxes to the earthly king. Once again Jesus examiners the situation closely while he examines a coin. Jesus responds by saying to give the king what is his and to give God what is his.

The third story also occurs in Matthew chapter 22 and is posed by an expert in the law after he is impressed by the prior response of Jesus. This lawyer seems to legitimately want to know what is the greatest commandment. This time there is no hesitation. Jesus answers that the greatest commandment is to love God with all your soul and all your mind. He emphasizes that this is the greatest commandment. But again without missing a beat, Jesus gives a close second commandment in that we are to love our neighbor as ourselves.

We do not wish to imply that we can capture the full impact of meaning of these three tests, but we do not wish to have certain elements pass us by. We first maintain that if Jesus can be tested then so too can we, especially like Peter when we seem to be on the precipice of a strong experience. In our first story we see that the heart of the gospel as it relates to our fellow human beings, does not stand in contrast to those standards which have gone before us. Next we see that ultimately the laws of God do not stand in opposition to the laws of mankind. Finally we see that the heart of the gospel equates serving God intently to loving our fellow human beings. When we assisted the least of these, we have been serving the Master in all his disguises as noted in the parable of the sheep and goats in Matthew chapter 25.

When Jesus followed Satan

Most of us are familiar with the rebuke that Jesus gave to Satan during Satan's temptation of Jesus. We recall the basics. After 40 days of fasting in the wilderness with wild animals present, Satan felt this would be an opportunity to tempt Jesus. We summarize briefly that the first temptation was to turn the stone into bread. Jesus will use the stone and bread comparison just 2 chapters later in the Sermon on the Mount in Matthew chapter 6. The appeal of Satan here is, as per his original approach in the Garden of Eden, to use facts as the starting ground and then appeal to the rationalization aspect. "If you are the Son of God........".

Parables and Paradox

Surely it is only rationale that God would want us to eat after we had already tested the limits of the human body and mind.

The next temptation in Matthew is with Jesus standing on the top of the temple. This time Satan uses the same rationale "If you are the Son of God...." This time he adds scripture. Jesus responds with more basic scripture. The final test follows along the lines of going to another high point and Satan offering all the kingdoms of the world for a little worship. Satan has no scripture this time to offer, but Jesus is quick to deliver his even in his food deprived state. Luke reverses the order of the last 2 temptations and adds the provision at the end of the temptations that the devil left until an opportune time.

What we may miss in this reading is that Jesus was not only led by the Spirit but also specifically to be tested by the devil. What is more though, is that Jesus willingly follows Satan on the second and third temptations. Furthermore the devil told Jesus what to do and he did it. Read Matthew 4:5. The devil took Jesus to the holy city and had him stand on the highest point of the temple. Again in verse 8 Jesus goes with Satan to a very high place to see the splendor of the kingdoms of the world.

Now the common interpretation in the temptation sermon is to show the power of Jesus to resist temptation and that we too can employ this tactic when we are tempted from the basics of life to the greatest materialism known to humankind. Well and good. Yet this story is meant to show that Jesus was able to resist temptation even when he was in an extremely weakened state. But in order for the rest of humankind to identify with the experience, we have to feel as if Jesus has been led very close to temptation so that we will feel the full identification of the experience and have the proper resources identified to escape the grasp of the devil. We have to feel that Jesus has walked in to a trap the same way the rest of us have.

Now, how do we get out of the trap? How do we extricate ourselves? First we must recognize the value of prayer and fasting and stop relegating that to yesteryear or the ultra religious. Next, we must be prepared with scripture to counter the temptations that come our way. Finally we must recognize that the biggest challenge all of us face is to overcome our rationalizations that begin with legitimate facts.

The human body can go 4 weeks at times without food. It can go up to one week without fluid. But our minds will not make a day or any fractionated portion of that day without our rationalizations. This is the key that is hidden in the temptation of Jesus. He has legitimate needs and legitimate opportunity. He does not need to prove to Satan that he is the Son of God. He does not need to prove it to himself. Both parties already knew that. Jesus simply avoids the rationalizations that reel most of us in.

The Temptations of Jesus and the Seven Deadly Sins

There is a school of thought which holds that we cannot fully identify with Jesus as the Christ unless we identify with him as a human being in every sense of the word. This includes being tempted and hence the temptation of Jesus is inevitable. All of the synoptic Gospels have the temptation of Jesus early in the ministry of Jesus. The Gospel of Mark has this temptation in the first chapter but does not specify what any particular temptation was. Both Matthew and Luke give very specific temptations in slightly different order, as we have detailed elsewhere. If we are to go with the theory that in order to identify as a human being that the Temptations of Jesus must represent all Temptations known to mankind, how do we put together a representative list of those Temptations?

Various parties have already compiled the list for us. Since we are dealing with a biblical perspective let us turn to the seven deadly sins described in Proverbs chapter 6 beginning in verse 16. These include haughty eyes, a lying tongue, hands that shed innocent blood, a heart that devises wicked schemes, feet that are quick to rush into evil, a false witness who pours out lies, and a man who stirs up dissension among brothers. These have some overlap with the traditional seven deadly sins that the early church has precautioned against. These include lust, gluttony, greed, laziness, wrath, envy, and pride. While there are distinctions between the two lists, there are certainly overlaps that are not too much of a stretch of the imagination. The question is how these two lists match up with the temptations of Jesus.

In the first temptation Jesus avoids the arrogance of being haughty by refusing to change something into something that it is not. That is, he will not change the stones into bread simply because he is hungry. This is, having something be a false witness to what it really represents.

He will not have innocent blood put at risk by throwing himself down from the high point of the temple because he understands the difference between suspending the laws of gravity and the application of a metaphor which Satan is purposely trying to literalize. Let the literalizer beware.

Keep in mind that if anyone was at the high point, Jesus was. We recall that immediately before the temptation both Matthew and Luke have both the spirit of God descending upon Jesus and the voice of God saying that this is my son whom I love and with him I am well pleased. Perhaps we as human beings experience our biggest Temptations after we have experienced the closest thing to God's presence that we may. we feel ourselves so full of power and might that we have a false sense that we can do no wrong.

It is, of course, false witness to worship the temporal or transitory for the eternal. That is the final temptation of Jesus in the Gospel of Matthew. Arguably this leads to the dissension among brothers. This, too, is inevitable if we spend our time in league with the source of strife, conflict, and dissension.

Arguably the seven deadly sins of the traditional early church are an attempt to fill in the gaps that the Proverbs scripture does not for the temptations of Jesus. Jesus is asked on the one hand to be gluttonous and get his bread. He may lust after the bread or even the kingdoms on earth. To do so would be to take the lazy way out. The pride that he is asked to exhibit or that Satan wishes to have is all too obvious. Is not envy part of the picture in the sense that we don't merely want something that someone else has but something that we feel we too deserve.

That leaves us only with wrath which might be interpreted as righteous indignation. If ever there was a time to have righteous indignation it would appear that Jesus in his encounter with Satan would be justified. We really don't have any evidence of that actually occurring. We do have Jesus quoting scripture. We do have Jesus redirecting Satan. We do have Jesus putting things in perspective. We do have Jesus telling Satan to go away. But no where do we have a display of wrath or even righteous indignation. Jesus avoids both the laziness of rationalization and the path of wrath. We might do well to use such responses as a measuring stick for our own responses to what we deem evil. Perhaps the flipside is that some of the causes that fly under the banner of Christian attack are actually measures that cause dissension among brothers as opposed to true evil. In these situations it is far more often the dissension that is the problem and not the preliminary condition.

Forgiveness

CHAPTER 5

Subject: The Birth of Forgiveness

No one questions that forgiveness is an integral part of the gospel. Some argue that it is a force more powerful than love. Certainly love cannot be complete or receive its full manifestation without the concept and practice of a deep forgiveness. On the one hand we can circumvent this section by noting that love, like forgiveness, ultimately comes from God. It would appear though, that God like expressions need to have some form of human representation in order for us to begin to understand and appreciate and perhaps ultimately express some of this ourselves.

The author of Matthew arguably sets the background for this human expression of forgiveness. In chapter 1 the author traces the genealogy of Jesus back to Abraham. What is most notable is that in addition to the patriarchs, David and a number of lesser figures, we have the mention of exactly four women. It is five if we count Mary, the mother of Jesus. We maintain that it is no small note that Mary is introduced in a way that makes her more important than Joseph. In verse 16 of chapter 1 we read that Jacob was the father of Joseph, the husband of Mary of whom was born Jesus who is called Christ.

Who are the other four women? Why are they listed? Is there any connection with Mary? The first woman mentioned in the genealogy is Tamar who was the mother of Perez and Zerah. To be clear these are children who were born of incest as we have detailed in our book on the patriarchs. The next is Rahab who was arguably the Madame of a brothel. The next is Ruth who was a foreign woman who arguably acquired her second husband by at least some form of solicitation if not more. Finally we have the mention of the wife of Uriah. With that mention we note several considerations. First the name of Bathsheba was not mentioned. Was this because to mention the actual name was still too suggestive or an actual reminder of a scandal or was there another reason? Please refer to our book on David to explore this concept further. We maintain it is no small measure that Bathsheba is referred to in the genealogy as the wife of Uriah.

While some have written on the purposeful mention of the use these women to diminish the potential scandal that Mary was an unwed mother, that is not our purpose here. Nor do we maintain the extreme opposite position that a virgin birth through Mary was to elevate the position of all women regardless of their background. We do maintain though that these women may well be mentioned in order to show a connection that some would have pre-supposed existed with Mary.

In fact Joseph himself believed that Mary had some type of illicit relationship before it was revealed to him that Jesus was conceived by the Holy Spirit. The evidence of this comes in verse 19 of chapter 1 of Matthew. We must keep in mind that while we the reader have already been told that the conception of Jesus was through the Holy Spirit, Joseph did not realize that in verse 19.

Rather we are told that he was a righteous man and did not wish to expose Mary to public disgrace and therefore was going to divorce her. This we maintain, was the first expression in the human flesh that

Jesus was both exposed to and would have been aware of. In other words, Joseph had already forgiven Mary even though he did not need to. The implication of that may be quite offensive to our ears today to suggest that we need to practice such a radical forgiveness Even to people who have not necessarily sinned against us. While we may have short changed Joseph all these years without realizing that forgiveness, we should also consider that Joseph had to practice that forgiveness to others all of his life who still believed in the scandal of his wife. This may be lost on us, but was certainly not lost on Jesus.

The Unforgiving Servant

The parable of the ungrateful and unforgiving and unmerciful servant comes immediately after the disciple Peter has asked Jesus how many times that he should forgive his brother. Peter throws out the number 7 as a reasonable response. But Jesus responds with 70 times 7 which was basically a symbol for infinity. But a number or even infinity is not as impressive as is a story. So Jesus tells the story of the Master who was settling accounts. One particular servant owed 10,000 talents. We are led to believe that this is a tidy sum that was insurmountable for that servant. The King orders him to be sold along with his wife and children and all possessions. The servant falls to his knees and begs for patience and that he will repay all. This moves the Master to compassion and he orders him released and the debt forgiven.

All would be good except that the servant with the large debt of forgiveness then goes out and demands full payment immediately from a fellow servant of a much smaller debt. He even grabs the servant by the throat. That second servant then fell to his knees similarly to the first, and repeats basically the first story. The social media of the day, namely fellow servants reported this behavior to the king. The infuriated king calls this first servant wicked because he would not pass the forgiveness on. Now his punishment will be much harder. This time it includes torture while he still must repay. The message of the parable is spelled out by Jesus in very clear terms. This is what will happen to us if we don't forgive our fellow human beings.

There is even an added rejoinder in the "live" version at the conclusion. The forgiveness must be from the heart. Keeping in mind that there are very few parables that come as a dire response to a question from the disciples, we have a message that is as succinct and at the same time incredibly clear with the extra provision to be from the heart. Jesus wanted that message of forgiveness to be loud and clear without ambiguity.

Brother Anger Paradox

Perhaps the ultimate paradox on the offensive that Jesus spoke is contained in chapter 5 of the Sermon on the Mount. The more we reflect on this gem, the more we realize not only it's simplistic blueprint for living, but also the richness of the style. The chapter begins with a series of positive attributes to aim for. You are blessed if you're poor in spirit, mourn, meek, hunger and thirst for righteousness, merciful, pure in heart, peacemaker, persecuted for righteousness, and have falsehoods related on behalf of the Master. These traits make us the metaphor of the salt of the earth, which is echoing the sands and dust of the earth metaphors that God used for Abraham when he was calling him.

Right after this Jesus mentions his next metaphor as the light of the world, we have a confluence of meanings. The ultimate New Testament metaphor is Jesus as the light of the world. Yet we are also called to be the light of the world. How do we accomplish this challenge? Jesus explains by making a bridge between the adjectives of how to be, as in the beatitudes, the metaphors of salt and light, and finally, action. The problem is that we may get lost in that transition because Jesus next mentions that he is not doing away with the Original Testament Law, but rather fulfilling it. He then notes that our righteousness must exceed the best known righteousness of the day, namely that of the Pharisees and other teachers of the law. Now we must confess that most of our impressions here are that we are already better than these guys because we are not hypocritical like them and accordingly pat ourselves on the back.

If we have that attitude, which to be clear, is not one of the beatitudes mentioned earlier, we are missing the boat. Jesus is actually trying to show the utmost respect for the Pharisees as those who not only knew the law, but kept it. What he wishes us to note is that action from the heart must go above and beyond the usual limited interpretations. Then he gives specifics. Old rule equals do not murder. New rule means don't even be angry with your brother or even call him foolish.

But the Master is not finished with his advancement of understanding. He says next that if we are offering our gift at the altar and remember that our brother has something against us that we are to go and make it right before we can have the proper attitude for worship. What we may not realize here is that Jesus is not focusing here on blame. Rather he is saying that regardless of who said or did what, that it is our duty even as the offended party to go to the offender and make it right. This is not a confrontation but rather a reconciliation. That was offensive and remains offensive to this day. But being on the offensive means that we put reconciliation above pride, blame, and even worship. Wow.

Mercy and the Unforgiving Servant

The question in the gospel arises as to whether there is unlimited forgiveness. On the one hand we would like very much to think that this is indeed the heart of the gospel. Yet there are paradoxes within the gospel that do hint at some limit. Take for example the story of the unmerciful servant found in Matthew chapter 18. The prelude to this begins in verse 21 when Peter asked Jesus how many times should he forgive his brother when his sins against him. The answer that Jesus gives is 70×7 which is affectively symbolic for infinity. Then Jesus proceeds to tell us a story in which very much there are limits to forgiveness.

The story involves a king who is representing the kingdom of heaven symbolically as stated by Jesus. This king wanted to settle accounts with all of his servants. Accordingly one of those servants who owed him an extreme sum which would be the equivalent of millions of dollars was not able to pay. The master, that is the king, ordered that he and his entire family be sold to repay the debt. There upon the servant begged for mercy and patience and a pledge that he would repay everything. At that point the master took pity and canceled the debt and let him go.

No sooner did this transpire that the forgiven servant proceeded to take a fellow servant and demand payment for a much smaller sum. He went so far to choke the servant and demand immediate payment. This fellow servant tried the same technique of asking for patience and mercy with a pledge to be paid back, but the wicked servant who himself has been forgiven showed no mercy.

The rest of the fellow servants did not like this predicament whatsoever. They reported to the master who became severely angry and called that unforgiving servant wicked and cast him into prison in order to be tortured. At this point we feel a certain comfort in the vindication and expression of justice. At first glance though this appears to be a contradiction to unlimited forgiveness. Consider the phrase in the Lord's Prayer "forgive our debts as we forgive" A closer look may reveal a different story. First of all we have the awareness that the first servant, who was ultimately unforgiving, owed a large sum of money. How did he come into this money and what has he done with that? Had he borrowed the money on false pretensions? Had he been a poor investor according to the parable of the talents that we have elsewhere? Had he extorted the money from fellow servants? Why is his family not included with the sentence in this case?

We do not have the answers for these rhetorical but necessary questions. What we do have is the suggestion that unless one is a forgiving person, he cannot himself experience an attitude of being forgiven. Perhaps this is the torture that is referred to at the close of the chapter. It is indeed an incredible torture for someone to live a life that is neither forgiving or accepting of forgiveness.

Forgiveness and Love

An interesting little debate can be engaging if the topic is which is the greater power, love or forgiveness. Of course, many will argue that you can't have one without the other. Perhaps the chicken and the egg conundrum as to which came first. Perhaps the story of the sinful woman who comes to wash the feet of Jesus in Luke chapter 7 may shed some light on each. The setup is a well to do religious leader who invites Jesus to dinner. We are then told that a woman who had lived a sinful life washed his feet with an expensive perfume. The religious host thinks to himself that Jesus should have picked up on her background. Jesus shows that intuitive perception by telling a story which illustrated that he indeed knew what her background was and what the host was thinking. He told a story about 2 people who owed money, with one of them owing 10 times as much as the other. Jesus wants the host to conjecture who would love the master more based on the amount forgiven.

If we are honest, we are offended that Jesus would imply that love is tied to the amount of debt forgiven whether it was actually monetary or figurative. When the host replies that he supposes, perhaps reluctantly, that the one with the most love would be the one who is forgiven the most. Jesus affirms this response. The seeming reluctance of the host may have been predicated on the fact that he sensed where Jesus was going with this. Jesus precedes to make the connection of the action of the woman washing his feet and anointing him with love and forgiveness. Our annoyance and offense may be easily missed in this story if we focus on the religious host missing the point. We are actually offended that both of the men who borrowed money from a moneylender were let off the hook with no seeming compensation. Were they irresponsible in obtaining a loan? Were they lazy and did not make enough to repay? Did the moneylender, who would have had clearly defined terms have a change of heart? We don't know, but our subconscious begs to know.

Let's back up and dissect the story a little more. The religious host calls the woman a sinner implying a label that is one of ongoing condemnation. Jesus never labels her a sinner but rather a woman who has many sins. The difference is both subtle and dramatic. Why does the woman weep without Jesus saying a word? Is she weeping for her sins? We maintain that she is weeping because Jesus is accepting her as she is without judging her or condemning her. Do keep in mind that we are told that the woman had lived a sinful life. "Had lived" is a tense that allows for the possibility that such a life is over, even before the encounter. She does still own her sins though until verse 47 where Jesus says her many sins have been forgiven. Again pay attention to the tense. They were already forgiven. Yet the woman still needs to have this affirmed in the next verse in the present tense. Jesus says that her sins are forgiven. We probably join the presumptive guests in wondering who is this who even forgives sins. Nowhere does the scripture explicitly state that it was Jesus who forgave her. That is our projection.

Furthermore, we do not have a license to sin more in order to be forgiven more and thus love more as some might derive from Jesus statements including "he who has been forgiven little loves little. All of us have plenty of sins that would qualify for big forgiveness if we simply humble ourselves while at the same time, employ our talent. Jesus closing statement to the woman is that her faith has saved her and to go in peace. What was her grain of mustard seed faith? It was a faith that Jesus would accept her without judging her. It was a faith put in action with being able to touch a man without having to please him. Someone once said that music is what happens between the notes. Forgiveness is what happens between the faith and the action and the acceptance of people who have wept and poured the oil of their soul unto one of the least of these human beings who represent Christ.

Forgiveness Formula

The Bible is a source that seems to lend itself to formulas. The problem is that some of those formulas just don't fit or stand up to scrutiny. For example, many like to use the formula that without the shedding of blood, that there is no forgiveness. Once again we see plenty of evidence in contradistinction from this in the gospels from Jesus himself. On several occasions he forgives people of their sins either as he is healing them or right before. The religious leaders of his time are offended by that just as some religious leaders are offended today because people were made whole without the application of the formula as they understand it. Furthermore most of us modern people are offended at the notion of an illness or infirmary being linked to a wrong doing as is at least indirectly implied. Of course modern medicine is replete with examples showing the connection with physical ailment and stress in our lives. The growing field of autoimmune disorders in fact has this concept as a cornerstone.

There are other formulas that don't completely square with the gospels and the message of Jesus. Many church formulas have elements of praise and thanks in them. We certainly are not decrying these useful concepts but just pointing out that they are not a perspective in the words of Jesus. Indeed his model prayer referred to the Lord's Prayer, is devoid of both of these concepts, although some will make a weak argument for the praise portion. There is no mistaking the message of forgiveness in that model prayer. We don't ask God for forgiveness. We tell him to forgive us. However the forgiveness is conditional. The tenses of forgiveness make the order clear. We tell God to forgive our past in the present or the future tense. But the conditions are only applicable if we have already forgiven others.

Jesus wanted to make this concept unmistakably clear such that it is the only concept from the model prayer that is expounded upon. No expounding on God's hallowed name. No expounding on the kingdom. No expounding on our daily needs. No expounding on temptation. To be clear, God's forgiveness is conditional. His love may be unconditional, but his forgiveness is very much conditional. If you forgive others who sin against you, your Heavenly Father will forgive you. But if you don't forgive others their sins, your Father will not forgive your sins. This message was not to be missed. But there are other powerful subtleties that we may miss in this. We have a power of free choice to deny the power of forgiveness, which is conditional and thus override the power of God's unconditional love. We also are to forgive even without the other person seeking forgiveness. This is offensive, but we do have a choice.

Parables and Paradox

Why Judas Hung Himself

Judas has been a convenient scapegoat for 2000 years. The reasons seem so obvious and seem to come literally out of the mouth of Jesus himself. We are all familiar with the story of the Last Supper which occurs in all 3 synoptic gospels as well as the gospel of John. This cohesion is somewhat rare and only serves to strengthen the vilification of Judas. When Jesus points out that the one who will betray him is the one who dips his bread with himself, Jesus, and then follows with the strongest of statements that it would have been better if this man had never been born, then the case is essentially closed, much as our own minds may be to additional discussion.

The story of the betrayal by Judas has been used by everything from justifying that suicide is wrong to the associated perpetual vilification of the Jews and along with them Judas who sought them out at the highest point of their leadership. This is certainly convenient, even if wrong. We feel allowed to sit in judgement over Judas as someone consumed by greed and taken over by Satan as several of the versions mention. In reality though we need to come to grips with the difference between the betrayal by Judas and the denial by Peter. If we sit in judgement without examining the full implications, then we also are culpable at some level.

The play Jesus Christ Superstar presents us with an opportunity to re-examine the motives and extend our reflections. Two generations after that play's inception we extend their story that perhaps Judas was not the complete villain he was made out to be for the better part of 2000 years. His statement "I don't want your blood money" sung in a most troubled and passionate voice to the Jewish leaders still conveys a strong sense of remorse. Even so we struggle with the reality that Judas seems deceptive and even in the gospel of John, we are told that Satan entered into Judas immediately after he shared bread with Jesus. Jesus adds the rejoinder to do his task quickly.

Now we transition from the conveniences of scapegoating to the inconvenience of scrutiny of scripture that may reveal inconsistencies and point to motives behind the message. As we examine these stories let us be careful to judge no one for their motives any more than we judge Jesus. Let us examine what is the meaning behind the story. The Last Supper is generally agreed to have happened at the traditional feast of unleavened bread that occurs with the Jewish Passover celebrating how Jewish lives were spared their firstborn when the angel came to deliver death to all those(mostly Egyptians) not displaying the proper sign. Luke chapter 22 says as much as do other versions. Here's where it gets a little tricky.

Luke chapter 22 also says that Satan entered into Judas Before the Passover. He then agrees to deliver Jesus to the authorities that would be apart from the crowds in order to not lose out to the popularity of Jesus. All well and good until we look at John chapter 13. There we are told that Satan entered Judas after Jesus gave him the bread to reveal who was the traitor. If we combine this version with the others, we see that neither Judas or any of the other disciples knew who it was who would betray Jesus. Some had the audacity to ask if was themself.

Somehow we have to reconcile these two versions of the same event. Did Satan enter into Judas on 2 different occasions? Does Satan come and go? Did Judas dismiss Satan after the first entering which is clearly defined as Before the Passover? Did Judas have an ulterior motive that went beyond greed and betrayal? Is it possible that he was trying to earn some money for the group since he was indeed identified as the treasurer? Was it possible that he believed that Jesus would use his power to extricate himself from the authorities? Even Jesus himself points to this opportunity to be rescued by God the Father by his angels in Matthew chapter 26 even as he is being arrested. What in the long run is really different from what Judas did compared to Peter or even the crowds? After all, turncoats (the crowd), denial (Peter), and betrayal (Judas) are merely shades of the same phenomenon.

Judas does, after all, repent when he realizes that things are not going to turn out like he expected. We don't really get any idea that the majority of the crowd ever repented. We know Peter repented and went on to do some heavy duty for the church. We might point out that Judas committed suicide and that suicide is a sin. The problem with this common interpretation is that nowhere in the Bible is suicide expressly forbidden. Arguably, in the case of Sampson at the end of his life, he prays to God to kill himself and in the process his enemies. We will need to place our bias, which sometimes indirectly translates into prejudice against the mentally ill, on hold, if we are going to come up with more potentially striking explanations.

Let's try forgiveness. That may be the distinction between Judas and Peter. Both betray in a sense, but Peter believes in the power of forgiveness which was something that Judas could not grasp. Many religious formulas site that there is no salvation unless there is repentance. However, repentance must be closely tied to forgiveness and the belief and understanding at least at some level that one is truly forgiven. Where we need to be careful as members of the crowd is what happens if we can't forgive Jesus? Arguably this is the somewhat immortal sin in that Judas cannot forgive Jesus for not living up to the image that Judas had in mind. We might do well to question our own motives when we have expectations that God does not match. Must we betray Jesus with the kiss of closeness when he does not live up to our expectations?

Stephen Harrison and Richard Huizinga

Who Really is Forgiven in the Prodigal

When we read the Prodigal, we make many assumptions that are not clearly defined while overlooking others. For example, we assume that the Prodigal was forgiven and perhaps that nobody else was. Let's examine the story again. Recall the setup in Luke chapter 15 where the prelude is searching for the lost. The first item is the lost sheep which was 1 out of 100. The second was the lost coin, which was 1 out of 10. Then we come to the Prodigal where it is 1 of 1, though arguably the older faithful and pious brother was somewhat lost as well.

The Living Bible makes the connection with the Prodigal and the first 2 stories above by noting by way of introduction in verse 11 "to further illustrate the point, he told them this story.....". Then Jesus launches into the Prodigal. We assume that the point was one of not giving up on something that was valued, and then we assume the forgiveness aspect. To be sure, this is strongly implied and we would do well to retain that meaning. In reality, the first 2 items were perhaps more valuable from an economic standpoint than they were valued. Also they were sought out, unlike the Prodigal. Again, there may be many ways to seek, and quite possibly the father sought in prayer day and night. That's the difference between humans and inanimate objects.

We must not overlook the possibility that the father wanted the Prodigal to return for economic sake. Certainly 2 working sons were more efficient than 1. Perhaps the elder faithful son was not even a good worker or manager. In fact, we have no evidence of that although we have strong evidence that the Prodigal was both a willing and hard worker. What if the younger son had been disturbed about the inequality of the birthright and not simply sowing his wild oats? What if the son had to forgive the father for that inequality? What if the Prodigal had to forgive the older brother for something he didn't even do, as in that type of arrangement, much as perhaps Joseph forgave Mary for something she didn't do?

What if the father forgave the older faithful brother? Keep in mind, that the father does expend energy to seek out the older pious brother, but does not for the Prodigal. It's all right there in verse 28. In fact, the father even went out to beg the older brother to celebrate the return. We should not overlook the possibility that the father was in the process of forgiving the older faithful brother. Nor should we overlook the possibility of the older pious brother forgiving the Prodigal or even his father.

Universal Emotions and Reconciliation

Shakespeare was the master at appealing to our emotions without necessarily having to name them. Yet for all the new words, idioms, and phrases that we can attach to Shakespeare, he did not conjure up a single new emotion. Rather his mastery was to sense those universal emotions and develop them into universal reliability. Knowing that Shakespeare used biblical stories for some of his inspiration and knowing that Jesus was no less a Master story teller, what does the Prodigal look like in regards to the universal emotions?

The surface and background of the Prodigal is about rejoicing over something lost. Jesus had an understanding of behavior economy and knew that one lost sheep with not only the economic factor, but also the emotional bonding had. Yet in each story of the lost sheep, lost coin, and lost son he gets right to the loss without dwelling on it. The sheep and coin losses lead to immediate extensive efforts to retrieve something perceived as valuable.

The Prodigal goes right to the losses as well. By the second verse the Prodigal has basically demanded his inheritance prematurely without so much of a discussion. The seemingly emotionless father at that times concedes the inheritance without debate or lecture or attempt to talk him out of it. Yet his emotions are very much there. Indeed the absence of their mention only further enhances them.

Every parent hearing this story has immediate multiple emotions. We are angry, irritated, and frustrated at the Prodigal, just as the religious leaders would have been at the son for being so brazen and selfish to demand his inheritance. We also, are meant to be irritated at the father for putting up no resistance or argument, as would also the religious leaders. It is one thing to lose an inanimate object which had no feeling. It is another to lose an animal where now we may well have emotional connection along with the economic. The Father has lost not only physical possessions but his son as well.

These first two stories set the stage for frustration, though no negative emotion is ever mentioned. Rather the owner in each of these stories sets out immediately to find the lost. With time lapse, we are then told immediately that the missing item is found. In both cases we are told of the immediate joy. In both cases we are told that the owner shared this joy immediately with friends and neighbors.

Let us not lose sight of the subtleties of the phrase friends and neighbors. There is meant to be a distinction. Friends may be neighbors and vice versa but we may indeed have neighbors that are not friends. Finding something that was lost has enough value to drive behavior economy to extend our outreach to those we come into contact with but don't necessarily have an intimate or even positive relationship with.

So now we have the subtle setup where there is frustration, followed by immediate joy, followed by shared rejoicing including just people in the proximity. Now we are set up to be frustrated in the Prodigal with some expectation of immediate restoration and shared joy. Except that we don't get immediate restoration. Rather, we get deeper frustration. Frustration at the Prodigal for his profligacy. Frustration with the father

Parables and Paradox

who did nothing to stop him and won't even extend the energy to seek out the Prodigal.

Now we are set up for the mixed emotions. The Pharisee in us says that it serves him right. He does not deserve the effort that we would give a lost sheep or even lost coin. The compassionate part of us feels the deeper frustration of a parent who does not know what to do when they sense the lostness of a child. The father, like us, is frozen as to what to do.

Then the Prodigal gathers his senses and returns home in a desperate sense. When the father sees him on the horizon the compassion that he feels immediately is driven strongly by pity. He knows either from a distant glance or from personal experience what the Prodigal has been through by his haggard appearance and penitent posture.

The father, uncharacteristically for men of his stature and generation, ran to meet his son. The Prodigal makes a brief confession, but his rehearsed speech is interrupted by the father. The father wishes to not only rejoice but to express that joy in a major feast of celebration. He has, no doubt, not only called for friends and family, but also for neighbors including those whom he himself has been estranged because everything about the Prodigal is meant to build on and extend the emotions of the earlier 2 stories.

We too are meant to be part of the lost. But if we are lost in the judgmental nature like the religious leaders, then we too will be standing outside of reconciliation. If we do not deal with the legitimate anger, frustration, and sense of fairness that the religious leaders legitimately had, then we too cannot have the total reconciliation with those with whom we are estranged, separated from, or just plain don't know or understand.

Ours is a fractured time of polar extremes in the political and social arena. To borrow from the medical jargon to extend this analogy, it not merely polarized, but it is bipolarized. Only by coming to grips with all emotions on all sides can we have effective reconciliation. We must deal with legitimate anger and frustration and a sense of fairness by balancing it not so much a vague love, but a compassionate forgiveness that is not deserved, but as we have dealt with elsewhere, will still be accounted for

Fatted Calf

What does the fatted calf symbolize in the prodigal? For that matter what does the prodigal symbolize for any culture? The fatted calf is symbolic of a most special occasion, a reunion. Even many internet definitions reference the story of the Prodigal as to the origin. The fatted calf represents a celebration of the highest order. Jesus notes elsewhere in one of his other parables that he is forgiven much can love much and even that he who is forgiven much has an opportunity to love more than he who is forgiven little. The fatted calf represents throwing the past into the past. Is this not the definition of forgiveness? Throwing the past into the past.

The celebration of the fatted calf represents all social get togethers today, family and beyond. It is a contractual arrangement. It is a celebration not solely because of what we share in common, but a sharing despite some differences. It is a sharing despite some wrongs that have transpired and a putting behind those elements for the sake of the ongoing relationship. Parties always seem to be so much in the Now. In reality, though, while there is an element that eliminates the past, there is simultaneously an element that is celebrating the agreement that the offending party will put extra effort into getting it more right the next time around. Yes there is momentous celebration, but it is also momentary.

The success of the celebration of the fatted calf is determined by 3 factors. These elements are the closeness of the relationship, the depth of the offense, and the extensiveness of the forgiveness. We are celebrating not only the so called Now moment of such feasting, but also the future which recognizes recompense for the offense to the extent possible, with an unexpressed, but definitely perceived feeling that that which cannot be fully recompensed will indeed be forgiven. To be sure, there is a past involved, but it is not the past of the offense. It is the past that says this is what we have always done. We do it because it works in ways that cannot be explained, but only experienced. It is paradoxical and offensive at the same time.

Jesus says in his model prayer the Lord's Prayer, that unless we forgive others that we cannot be forgiven. This is because resentment of offense is a space occupying lesion that leaves no room for anything else. God is not a little child who will give us what we want if we give him or someone else what they want. The log in our eye referenced in the Sermon on the Mount is a grudge that we need to eliminate first in order to experience the opportunity to relieve someone else's burden.

Metaphors in John and The Gift of Forgiveness

Metaphors figure prominently and are pervasive throughout the gospel of John. This begins right off the bat with the metaphor of the light of the world that shines in the darkness and came from God and was God. This mystical light of the world will be balanced by more practical metaphors throughout the Gospel of John. As early as the first chapter we will also see Jesus referred to as the Lamb of God who takes away the sin of the world.

The blend of the heavenly light of the world will be balanced throughout the gospel by practical earthly metaphors that people of all times can relate to. Always looming in the background is the challenge of Jesus confronting the religious leaders of his times. At times though there is also the seeming challenge of confronting the familiar and disavowing ourselves from that.

The first such an example we might see is the first miracle Jesus recording at a wedding feast in which his mother approaches him when the hosts have run out of wine. Jesus senses correctly that his mother is asking for a miracle which he is not prepared to do at that time based on some internal clock that tells him his time has not yet come. Yet his mother realizes that he will honor the Commandments and therefore honor his mother by performing the request.

The next big story is when a prominent Jewish leader goes to the light of the world at night time sincerely searching for answers. He is told that he must be born again which metaphor he does not understand. During this encounter we get the promise of eternal life for those who believe. We also get the extension of the light metaphor. The pattern of people coming to Jesus has continued and will do so in the next chapter as well.

In the fourth chapter of John the woman of ill repute will go to Jesus while he was at the well hoping for a drink of water. In the story the humanity of Jesus is not hidden but rather we are told that he is tired from the journey and sat down. As tired as he may be humanly the divine powers of clairvoyance have not abandoned him and he is still able to see into the woman's background. He ends up displaying very human compassion for this woman and in so doing loses his sense of hunger and thirst as any human might do when they are caught up in a worthy project.

Now with a very human compassion on the line Jesus will seek out his first person to heal. This person in fact is paralyzed and cannot go to Jesus as we see in chapter 5. This ultimately provokes a confrontation with those who wish for the rules to be followed in the strictest sense on the Sabbath even if it means denying a much sought for healing.

Parables and Paradox

The next big miracle will be the feeding of the 5000 which serves as the backdrop for the bread of life metaphor later in the chapter. It also serves as a point of distinction between believers and nonbelievers. Accordingly many people begin to fall away after this testimony and the rest of the book of John becomes laden with confrontations with the Jewish religious leaders.

Along the way we will see some additional healings in which we reference the light of the world once again. We will also have the metaphor of the shepherd and his flock. Furthermore he was show some very human emotion of weeping before he raises a good friend from the dead. He will then perform the very human act of washing his disciples feet and shortly thereafter comforting his disciples. Shortly thereafter he will give the story of the true vine and the branches.

In his dying moments he will show compassion for his mother that may not have been particularly evident throughout his life. He will put his beloved disciple John in charge of her well-being. After his death he will appear to Mary Magdalene and provide very human reassurance to her as he does later to the disciples. The final charge that he is given to the disciples after he has risen solidifies the combination of humanity and divinity.

In John chapter 20 Jesus will appear to the disciples with the simple admonition for them to have peace. He will show them the very visible wounds from the crucifixion of trying to be something more than human. After wishing them peace again Jesus inspires them with the Holy Spirit. Then they are given the most important gift that human beings can have in dealing with each other. That is the gift of forgiveness.

In conclusion the humanity of Jesus, in the gospel of John, may have been obscured by ignoring the physical birth unlike the synoptic Gospels. The oppressed of any era may relate to his broad confrontations with the leaders of his time. The miracles however become obscured without the metaphors. In the end he combines his humanity with his divinity not simply with the gift of the Holy Spirit but with the gift of forgiveness.

Inclusion

CHAPTER 6

Inclusion

While it is always possible to read more info a parable than was intended, we might do well to consider that we have a God given mind for which we have a commandment to use all of it to love God. Accordingly we bring up the idea of inclusion which was not foreign to Jesus himself. This concept cannot be disavowed in the prodigal. It is quite possible that the father knew the son would be exposed to much more than riotous living. He might well be exposed to different ways of thinking or different philosophies. He may well be welcoming home someone he knows will introduce new thoughts and ideas and challenges the system just as he has challenged the system before. No matter. He is embraced.

If we reflect further we cannot discount the possibility that the father had accomplished his own experience that was not unlike that of the prodigal. Those who see the father as representing the Heavenly Father or God will no doubt be offended. We remind them of Jesus own parable of the unjust judge in which he compare his own father, God, to an unjust judge. We can dismiss too easily the idea that the father identified more all along with the prodigal more than the older brother, but this may well be what the elder faithful brother was referencing when he was talking to the father about the prodigal and called him "that son of yours" It is too easy to think of the faithful son as envious and not perceiving that his father loved him equally.

Mark's Perspective

Is it possible to surmise the perspective on the gospel of Mark without knowing much about the book? From the first chapter dramatizes key connections for Jesus. Even the first verse emphasizes good news, and that Jesus is the Messiah, and the son of God. Both the Original Testament through Isaiah, and the New Testament through the prophet John the Baptist point to Jesus. While John preached to the down trodden for repentance for the forgiveness of sins, Jesus portends something greater. Jesus indeed is noted to pick up where John left off when the latter went to prison. All of this along with his baptism and the spirit of God descending on him the voice of God making the connection that Jesus is his son and that he is well pleased with him occurs in the first 15 verses. Arguably everything is anticlimactic after that.

Nonetheless, he has been recognized as a son of God and so it would be appropriate to display his authority. So he proceeds to the temple where he is recognized as someone who teaches with authority in contradistinction from the usual religious authorities. He also teaches inclusion and challenges authority and guidelines for guidelines sake. His first healing is on the Sabbath to relieve a man with an impure spirit.

Perhaps the unclean spirit is a metaphor for the rest of us that we may miss too easily. Jesus branches out from his own roots of healing in a religious setting to healing of family of the disciples, then the community at large including the sick and once again the demon possessed. These healings are presaged by being alone after the baptism and once again by being alone after a series of healings. That private time is used to regenerate his energy for more preaching in synagogues and driving out more demons.

Next Jesus is approached by a leper who wishes to be healed. The leper requests to be healed if Jesus is willing. The NIV and ERV make Jesus to appear either indignant or angry. The KJV and MSG totally emphasize the compassion of the healing, which seems to be more fitting with what follows. Jesus proceeds to heal him but charges him to tell no one except the priest as Moses commanded. This only seems to motivate the grateful man even more who then proceeds to tell everyone who comes near, which Jesus had to have the foresight would happen. While this motivated Jesus to stay out of towns, the people still found him.

Even so, the next chapter finds Jesus having entered another synagogue very much in a town. Just as he began the first chapter with a healing that challenged the norms by healing on the Sabbath, this time he forgives sins before healing a paralyzed man.

The rest of this chapter is spent challenging conventional norms such as eating with sinners, fasting, and doing basic measures on the Sabbath, like getting some grain. This basic process translates once again to a healing on the Sabbath as the first healing in chapter 3. Jesus proceeds to heal many including demons which he admonishes not to tell anyone. Following this Jesus commissions the disciples to preach and cast out demons. Interestingly, they don't do anything else. Finally chapter 3 is concluded by distancing himself from his family just after he has once again distanced himself and distinguished himself from the religious authorities.

Chapter 4 has several parables and then concludes with Jesus calming a storm. This seems to be a prelude for calming a demon possessed man with many demons in chapter 5. This man wants to follow Jesus, but this time Jesus charges him to actually go and tell how much the Lord has done for him. Notice, here that Jesus does not say how much Jesus himself had done, but the man translates the statement by stating that Jesus had done much for him, which effectively made this man the first to equate Jesus with God. Given that chapter 6 has synagogue healings and that chapter 5 included a healing for family of religious leaders, this makes every chapter of the first 6 about a healing in the synagogue or something connected with it.

Jesus continues to challenge and be challenged by the religious authorities in chapter 7. His first story points out that what defiles people is not what goes into them but rather what is in their hearts. That message should not be lost upon us when he challenges the Greek woman from Syrophoenicia who wanted to be healed. Jesus seemed to be making this woman work for her healing much as he challenged the woman who touched his coat in chapter 5. These are persistent people and one must contrast this with those claiming to be his family earlier who do not seem to have the heart to persist in their efforts. They wish to identify with him, but Jesus seems to identify with those who are sincere and in need.

Mark is very much a symmetrical book where the first 8 chapters have direct and confrontational measures with religious authorities amidst a wide array of healings. The pivotal chapter 8 begins with Jesus feeding 4000 people only to be followed by a demand from the religious authorities that they be shown a sign? The next healing involves a blind man who is healed in 2 stages. These healings seem to serve as metaphors for the religious leaders. They are blinded to the authority of Jesus and paralyzed in their thought and tradition.

The second half of Mark will be filled with more direct confrontations with the religious authorities and punctuated with some teachings on life and less healings. Just as there was drama in chapter one about the heaven connection, chapter 9 will begin with the transfiguration with Moses and Elijah present with Jesus. As much as each chapter thereafter has a confrontation, challenge, and distancing from the religious authorities, there is paradoxically a message of inclusion contained in the second half. This is done after the metaphor of salt representing the old guard and its need to be replaced is issued at the end of chapter 10. The old guard will challenge Jesus authority repeatedly throughout the rest of the book until his death.

During this time, Jesus will emphasize the kingdom of inclusion by acknowledging several times the importance of children and their attitudes. He will emphasize that the kingdom of heaven is for the poor in spirit who are willing to sacrifice all, be it their possessions or their attitudes. A Woman will be acknowledged who washed his feet in chapter 14. Women in general will be acknowledged when they are the first to witness the resurrection of Jesus. Basically Mark has turned everything from the first 8 chapters on its head by challenging conventional authority. While he heightens those challenges in the second half, he elevates the status of women, children, and the poor.

If we make the gospel of Mark out to be a gospel of exclusion against religious authorities and the like, we will miss the heart of the gospel. The gospel is one of inclusion. Religious people have their opportunity and are even included in the healings. A rich man is the only one in the entire gospel that Jesus is said to have loved as found in Mark10:21. Finally while he acknowledges that the kingdom of heaven belongs to people who are childlike, the only adult that he notes as close to the kingdom of heaven was one of the religious leaders who came to question Jesus as to what was the greatest commandment. That leader once again brought the heart into the equation by noting that we need to love God with all our heart and to love our neighbor as ourself. That is the essential message of Mark.

Stephen Harrison and Richard Huizinga

Good Samaritan

Most of us with church backgrounds probably have a fairly accurate recollection of the parable of the Good Samaritan. Ostensibly it is about a despised foreigner who stopped to help someone who had been robbed, beaten, and left for dead.

We don't know what the nationality or ethnicity of the wounded individual was, though we are given some clue that he may have had a fairly strong connection with the Jewish faith as we was traveling between two holy towns, Jerusalem and Jericho. We are meant to sense the religious connection even stronger by being told that first a priest passed by and later a Levite, who was also very religious. However, they both went out of their way to avoid contact with the injured man, who quite likely shared a fair amount of religious DNA.

Then, of course, the hero the Samaritan arrives on the scene. He offers first aid, puts the man on his own donkey, which made his own journey more arduous, risky, and time consuming. He takes him to the place of local hospitality which word shares entomological roots with our word hospital. This was the best place to go to get well, but then, like now, it cost money. As the Samaritan travelled alone, I believe we are meant to feel that he left a substantial amount of money when he pulled out the 2 silver coins in order to provide ongoing care when the Samaritan departed. The parable ends by the Samaritan promising to repay any additional expenses that may be accrued and not covered by the silver left.

Let's break down some measures here in terms of the logistics. First let's begin with the title of the parable. Jesus, of course, did not label his parables. Furthermore, he did not even call the Samaritan good. Rather, that was left for future generations who might pretend that they have no prejudice when they utter phrases like "good" (fill in your own minority).

The minute we introduce the term "good" we cannot help but read into the story that most of the rest of the Samaritans were bad.

Let's try the phrase "the good Mexican immigrant who may not have been fully legal" in order to capture a bit of the prejudice. Jesus does not use that terminology. Rather, he understood that there was some history there that had led to estrangement and even despising. He realized that most of that was predicated on not having enough shared experience, whether or not it be suffering or joy.

Jesus himself is reminded of the separation when he asks a Samaritan woman at a well for a drink of water. The woman replied that Jews don't ask Samaritans for a drink or anything else for that matter. Jesus alludes to Eternal life or living water that he can give the woman. He notes that he is aware of her past with many men but he makes no judgement on her. Next he points out some differences in their religious positions and briefly even seems to point to the superiority of the Jewish religion. That is, he notes shortly thereafter, not the point. Rather the zenith of belief and expression comes when all believers will worship the Father in spirit and truth.

The woman who has had the microcosm of her life revealed to her and the essentials of the gospel of truth revealed to her wishes to demonstrate her belief in such spiritual matters by noting that she is looking forward to the coming of the Messiah who will explain everything. When Jesus calmly replies that he is that Messiah, it is the earliest revelation by Jesus himself by far in any gospel. Let us not lose sight that it comes to a woman. It comes to a sinner. It comes to someone who doesn't believe correctly. It comes to a foreigner, a Samaritan.

Meanwhile, our mind has many questions about the logistics. How did the Samaritan earn his money? He seemed to leave it all with the innkeeper, but we don't really know that. As mentioned earlier, we really don't know what the background of the injured party was. We don't know about the attackers. Perhaps they were Samaritans, not the "good" type. We don't know the background of the innkeeper. Was he going to trust a Samaritan to return as promised. The point here is that virtually none of this matters. What matters is that whoever lives by the challenge in Matthew 25 and answers the need of the moment, has fulfilled the spirit of the gospel.

The parable is framed with a real life event. It begins with an expert in the law of the day who wants to test Jesus by asking what he must do to inherit eternal life. We don't know if he believed that there was eternal life, was actually seeking some insight, just testing, or making light of the concept. We would perhaps be careful to avoid presumptions. After all, Jesus takes the question seriously enough to answer concisely the heart of the commandments, "love God with all your heart, soul, mind, and strength and love your neighbor as yourself." The lawyer, though wants to justify himself. Jesus, on the other hand, wants justice. At the end of the parable he asks the lawyer who was neighbor to the injured man. The lawyer answers succinctly "the man who had mercy." Jesus could have replied "exactly "which would have been a succinct and curt response indicating that the man was right. Except that the man wasn't right. Jesus said go and do likewise. The man was not right by knowing the intricacies of the law. He was not right until he showed mercy and inclusion to the unknown and perhaps undeserving victims.

Specific Healings

We find it interesting that before the Sermon on the Mount that there are no specific healings in Matthew. Rather, after the temptation of Jesus we have a brief mention that he healed a variety of people with difficult to treat conditions from many different areas. After the Sermon on the Mount we see some more specific healings. The first such was a man with the disease of leprosy which left him suffering from his condition as well as a social outcast. That leper appeals to Jesus noting that if Jesus wills it, he can make the man clean and cured. Jesus does so by saying first that he is willing. Then he reaches out and touches him.

This had to be incredibly shocking and offensive to the many people who were witnesses, right after the Sermon on the Mount. Here they have just witnessed one of the most amazing oral speeches for living that has ever been heard and then the man who uttered it is going to break the rules he just said he came to fulfill and touch someone unclean. Now given that we are told that large crowds were present, it seems a little peculiar that Jesus then tells him not to tell anyone that he has been healed, but to go and show himself to the priest and do the rituals to verify healing that Moses commanded. A suspension of the rules, but not quite.

The specific healings continue next with Jesus healing the servant of a centurion, even at a distance. The significance is not simply one form of authority recognizing another, but rather Jesus responding to the needs of someone who stood for all that was suppressing the land of Israel. Jesus then heals his first identified female, namely the mother-in-law of Peter. Now that we have the first specific healings identified as an unclean man, the symbolic foreign oppressor, and a woman, we can go on to the potential offense of a healing. First we have another interlude where Jesus will cast out demons from 2 wild men. For this Jesus will be asked to depart from the area. People may not like demons, but someone who can control them is frightening.

So now we have the setup to go to his own town. There he will encounter a paralyzed man. He tells the man to take heart because his sins are healed. This is beyond offensive. It is blasphemy, at least according to some of the teachers. Jesus is able to sense their thoughts and hearts and calls them out on it. He then goes on to establish that he has the authority to forgive sins as he will evidence by healing the paralyzed man.

The question here is who is really paralyzed here. The teachers were certainly not capable of movement from their rigid positions. Are we to read into this a connection between illness and sin? Now we are back to offending the modern reader. We can over read these measures at the risk of overlooking the first miracle done in his own town in Matthew. Forgiveness is a miracle available to all of us that makes absolutely no sense and so offends our moral dignity. It is undeserved. This first documented New Testament occurrence of forgiveness involves movement and liberation, but not death, except a death to an outmoded way of thinking.

Healings and Strange Proclamations

The ninth chapter of Matthew and the eighth chapter of Luke and the fifth chapter of Mark share several similarities in healings and concepts. All of them have the story of the ruler of the synagogue who requests for Jesus to heal his daughter who is dying. In each person that story of healing is interrupted by a woman who is seeking to be healed after 12 years of the flow of blood. As a physician, I am particularly troubled about some of the details given by the version in Mark. There we are told that the woman had been bleeding for 12 years and had suffered a great deal under the care of many doctors and has spent all she had and yet instead of getting better grew worse. I cannot imagine anything worse being said about a physician's reputation that would make him sound worse than failing to cure a poor woman after 12 years while she suffered all along and spent all her money on something that did not result in a cure.

The story is revealing because it shows Jesus taking the time to heal this bereft woman who has suffered long despite the fact that he is on his way to help a religious leader whose daughter is dying. The woman, though, wants to achieve the healing as inauspiciously as she can and surmises that all that she needs to do is to touch Jesus's coat from behind. Indeed she does just that and is instantly healed. More importantly, it is noted that she was freed from her "suffering" that she felt in her body as though the two may have been related but were indeed separate phenomena.

We are most likely offended by what happened next because Jesus immediately questioned who it was the touched his clothes because he sensed that power had gone out of his body. Now the woman who had been incredibly secret or furtive but bold is troubling and she trembles in fear. Jesus however wishes to acknowledge her faith and says to her to go in peace and be freed from her suffering because her faith has healed her. In other words, when she felt freed in her body from her suffering, that act was not necessarily complete until Jesus confronted her spirit and performed the entire release.

This shows the strong connection between bodily healing and spiritual healing while at the same time some subtle differences. While we are distracted momentarily from the offense that we might feel at Jesus for confronting the woman, we are immediately taken back to the story of the ruler and his daughter. Messengers have arrived to deliver the news that the daughter is dead and that there is no point in bothering the Master. Jesus of course is not deterred. No point of bothering the Master with the dead. But that is exactly what the Master wants – to be bothered after death. Indeed, he can only reveal a new paradigm after the death.

We are now taken from a chapter where 12 was a key number representing the number of years that the woman suffered as well as the age of the daughter as well as the number of disciples in Jesus's contingent.

When he goes to perform the healing he does not have anyone follow him except Peter James and John. Jesus does not stop his mission of healing even when people laugh at him as in this instance. Rather he commands the girl who is dead to get up which she does indeed and walks around.

While the ninth chapter of Matthew includes the same two stories it is framed by two other healings. The first one is performed in Jesus hometown where he heals a man that is paralyzed. Jesus, however, will not heal the man until that man knows that his sins are forgiven. Jesus of course is making a point for the leaders noting that he has authority on both heaven and earth and proceeds to perform the physical healing as well. We are naturally drawn into the offense that the rulers give when they fail to recognize the true authority of Jesus, but we may miss some measures intended for us. The real paralysis comes in a way of thinking that we have a certain lack of knowledge or spiritual insight and we will miss things that are closely connected with us because of that paralysis of thinking.

We also may overlook the connection between physical and spiritual healing. Later in the chapter Jesus will heal the blind simply because they believe that he is able and openly acknowledge their blindness.

Matthew then ends his chapter with the healing of the demon possessed man. For both Mark and Luke this healing is the first that occurs in the respective chapters listed. Luke sets the stage for the healings by telling the parable of the sower as well as the lamp on a stand followed by somewhat of a rejection of his mother and brothers and then the calming of the storm. What Mark and Luke both have included at the conclusion of the demon possessed healing is an indirect acknowledgment that Jesus and God are one in the same. Read verses 19 and 20 of Mark chapter 5 and then verse 39 of Luke chapter 8. After the man is healed Jesus instructs him to return home and tell how much God has done for him. Following that the man proceeds to go all over town telling how much

Jesus had done for him. The man has subtly interpreted that Jesus is God making a proclamation well before Peter's acknowledgment that Jesus is the Christ the son of God.

We are instinctively offended by this being the first documented acknowledgment of Jesus as God because we would rather have the great Peter be that individual as opposed to someone who had been demon possessed. We may be offended that the people of that area ask Jesus to leave after such a healing but we ourselves do not recognize the many many faces of Jesus and the unlimited power of healing. This healing occurs when people are paralyzed in body and mind and spiritually. This healing occurs even if people laugh at God. This healing occurs when people believe such as the woman and when they believe it is too late such as in the healing of the rulers daughter. This is the true paradox of total and complete healing.

Parable of the Sower: Jesus' most Basic Parable

Many a fine sermon has been preached on the parable of the sower. This basic parable is found in the three synoptic Gospels of Matthew Mark and Luke. Indeed it is essentially the most fundamentally basic parable in the words of Jesus himself. All of the gospels listed include a similar statement found in verse 13 of chapter 4 of the Gospel of Mark in which Jesus basically asks the disciples who don't understand initially the meaning of the parable that how would they understand any parable if they did not get this very basic one. If we're honest with ourselves we are embarrassed for the disciples who had to wait to ask Jesus in private what's the meaning of this most basic parable was.

The farmer of course represents Jesus himself as he spreads the word. The seed indeed is the message of truth as represented in repentance, reconciliation, and love. Jesus later explains that the first seed that was sown along the path and was snatched up by the birds represents those who hear the message and then are sidetracked by Satan. The next seed that is sown by the rocks represents those who hear the message eagerly initially but do not have any root that will allow them to continue to grow in the face of adversity. Jesus is quite clear with this second group that their adversity comes because they do wish to believe in the world. This adversity is once again easy to attribute to the adversary Satan but the scripture does not actually indicate that as the source. This allows that we may receive adversity at the hand of God or at least allowed by God as in the book of Job.

The next seed that does not thrive is the seed that is sown by the thorns. Jesus again is quite clear here in that the reason for failure to thrive is because of the fixation on the worries of this life along with the deceitfulness of wealth and the desires for other items. Once again our own minds naturally attribute these distractions to Satan but once again that is not what Jesus actually says when he is spelling out the meaning of this parable to the unwitting disciples. These distractions, including wealth, may well be legitimate pursuits created initially by God. For sure it is about priorities, but we do not get to have the clear distinction that we would like to have here between good and evil. Accordingly at some level that is offensive to us. Perhaps we have even choked others with our own theology that is not necessarily God's theology when we need to choke on our own theology.

Now all that we have left is the good seed, the good receptive soil, and the good farmer. Once again the meaning of this is so obvious that we pat ourselves on the back and slap the disciples in shame for not knowing. If however, the farmer represents Christ himself, we are forced to struggle with why the farmer wasted seed in areas that he would have known would not have been fruitful.

Of course one strong possibility here is that we ourselves are represented by the farmer. We do not have a choice as to where we sow the seed of truth but only a duty or obligation to provide an opportunity for growth. The seeds that were sown were for inclusion. We do not determine where we sow or what the results will be. Our only duty is to make an effort.

Nicodemus

The story of Nicodemus as portrayed in John chapter 3 is one of those stories which we are pretty certain that we get but that really should probably offend us. At face value it appears to be the story of one of the learned rulers of Jesus day who may be ultimately trying to trap Jesus by something that Jesus says. Let us keep in mind that at the conclusion of this first encounter that we hear of with Nicodemus that Jesus gives us the famous verse about eternal life found in John 3:16.

Let us give Nicodemus the benefit of the doubt and that he recognized that Jesus was a teacher from God because he performed miracles. Jesus follows that statement that no one can see the kingdom of God unless he is born again. We must be careful from what follows next to avoid using the retrospective lens to infuse meaning or lack of awareness on Nicodemus part. Most scholars feel that Nicodemus knew that when Jesus discussed being born again that he was not talking about a physical birth and so he is legitimately probing.

We are set up to see Nicodemus as one of the many Jewish leaders of his time who did not get Jesus real message from the moment we meet Nicodemus because he seems insecure and that he must come to Jesus at night time when none of his colleagues or the general public can see him. It is possible that we might even reinforce this notion with the closure of that encounter in which Jesus says that everyone who does evil hates the light and will not come into the light for fear that his deeds will be exposed in John chapter 3 verse 20. We must keep in mind though that Jesus follows this statement quickly what is the final verse of the encounter by noting that whoever lives by the truth comes into the light so that it may be seeing plainly what he has done has been done through God.

Nicodemus is trying hard to find the truth. He has seen the light of the world that shines through not only his darkness of the cover of night but all of the darkness of the world. As the passage further notice Jesus was not sent to condemn the world but to save the world. This saving of the world implies a universal truth, to be inclusive. In order for that truth to be understood, our institutions that represent our best understanding of truth such as Nicodemus represented must be challenged and born again in a new light. Arguably Nicodemus does capture the truth and try to present a portion of it to his colleagues in John chapter 7 in order for those colleagues not to prematurely judge Jesus. He then appears after the crucifixion to secure the body and properly embalm it. Ultimately Nicodemus represents an element that is trying to secure the truth and is willing to challenge the dogma of his day.

Do You Love Me Simon Peter?

Most of us are familiar with the post resurrection encounter of Jesus with the disciples as illustrated in the gospel of John. The flighty Peter has come from the ignominy of the three denials about his connection with Jesus. Jesus has instructed the unsuccessful fishermen disciples on adjusting their nets for success. The success was instantaneous and dramatic. The gospel of John spares no opportunity to have Peter look poorly and be second fiddle to the disciple that Jesus loved. That latter disciple tells Peter that he has identified the risen Jesus. The overzealous

Parables and Paradox

Peter abandons his friends and leaps out of the boat to go to Jesus. Jesus meanwhile waits on the shore with a charcoal fire going and some fish already on it. While no doubt this could have sufficed to feed them all, it would appear that Jesus wants them to utilize their own resources. Ah yes, but perhaps the ruse is to make Peter look a little worse. The man who has abandoned ship for glory returns to the ship.

After a fish breakfast Jesus is ready to put Peter to the test. The common interpretation is that Jesus must ask Peter if he loves the Lord 3 times in order to parallel the 3 times that Peter denied knowing Jesus. This is tidy but makes it sound like Jesus is simply keeping score like any earthling and demanding payback. Three times Jesus asks Peter if he loves Jesus. Three times Peter responds "yes Lord you know I love you." The first time Jesus instructs Peter to feed his lambs, that is the lambs of Jesus. The second time, he instructs Peter to take care of the Master's sheep. The third time vexes Peter but he responds the same with the additional phrase that the Master knows everything. Jesus responds once again for Peter to feed his sheep.

Let's examine further what the challenges of Jesus represent. He is not trying to even the score from the denial. He is pairing up love with action. He does not doubt that Peter loves him. Nor do we see any evidence that Jesus was upset with Peter. Rather it is a systematic instructional to Peter as to how to demonstrate his love. First he is to feed those young in the faith as represented by feeding the lambs, which by definition are less than one year old. The sheep represent the more mature believer who could still fall away like sheep do. Like Peter did. Like the parable of the one lost sheep out of a 100. Finally Peter is to nourish the mature in addition to protecting them. All of us, like Peter are commanded to show our love for the Lord by action. This is ultimately conveyed in another sheep and goat story told in Matthew 25. "I was hungry and you fed me......".

Stephen Harrison and Richard Huizinga

Rich Young Ruler Parable or Real Life

The meaning of the rich young ruler seems so obvious as to the meaning of being consumed by greed and wealth that we may overlook some of its implications for us today. The story is found in all 3 synoptic gospels in much the same format. Each version may present some of the slant that pervades the particular gospel. We will employ Mark as the most rudimentary version while recognizing the additional perspectives from the other 2.

In Mark we see both the sense of urgency along with some humility right off the bat. The man begins his encounter with Jesus by running up to him, something very atypical for a religious leader of the times. He also fell to his knees in what seems a legitimate sign of humility again. Jesus seems to appreciate this rich young man because he is a rarity in Mark as being singled out as someone whom Jesus loved. Luke is the only gospel that designated the man as a ruler. Luke is also the only gospel that has Jesus tell the man to his face how hard it is for a rich man to enter the kingdom of God.

All 3 gospels play on the word good. Both Mark and Luke reference Jesus as good teacher. In Matthew the question is framed what good thing must the man do to get eternal life. If we substitute the word acquire for get, then we have some additional insight perhaps into the man's perspective. The other gospels note the question framed as to what has to be done to inherit eternal life. Putting them all together we appear to have a rich man who not only inherited his wealth, but was used to getting what he wanted for the right price. Jesus begins by flipping the question and turning the tables such that the issue becomes what is good. In all versions Jesus points out that there is only One who is good.

Jesus lists a synopsis of the 10 commandments which the man maintains that he has kept since he was before the age of accountability.

Now we naturally wonder if the man truly has kept all the commandments since his early days, but that is not the point. Jesus grants the man this. Was the man seeking some attention for that performance or was he truly searching for something missing? The point here was not to question his motives but to point out what his deficit still appeared to be, namely that he had too much faith in his possessions. This is a subtle but potentially important distinction in that it was not so much about the extent of the possessions, but rather that those possessions possessed him.

But what did he actually possess? For sure there was the materialism that he appears to have inherited and can use to influence others. What is it that he cannot ultimately give up. Besides the possessions we must consider that the man could not stand to give something to people who perhaps did not deserve it. Perhaps he could not fathom the idea of being a follower as opposed to being a leader. Perhaps he could not give up certain belief systems which would make him more easily identified with us today. Whatever the case, the man walks away from what he was seeking, namely eternal life.

Rich Young Ruler's True Identity

The rich young man has been challenged to give away everything that he possesses and at the same time everything that possesses him. Of course we all know that the rich man walked away from his encounter with Jesus seemingly walking away from eternal life. We are told in all versions that the man walked away sad. In Mark we again have his basic but picturesque description. The man's face fell. Then he walked away sad. Jesus has offered this man perfection as we read in Matthew that if he wants to be perfect, he must sell his possessions and give to the poor. Anachronistically we think that the man has turned down the offer not simply of a lifetime but of an eternal lifetime.

This encounter though is not meant to read anachronistically as an infomercial in which the eternal life is offered for a limited time only. We would do well to examine the Eternal not as an endless future that replaces earthly time but is still replete with the earthly possessions. That is a rather simplistic way of thinking and we miss the application for our own lives if we think that the man was a fool simply because he didn't realize that he was giving something he considered good to get something perfect forever.

Let's delve into something deeper here; let's examine some more practical implications of Jesus challenge to the rich man. In no version is the man told to give everything away. Read them all again. He is told to sell everything. We must consider who he would sell to. Other rich men would be the biggest contenders here. Jesus recognizes this pragmatic matter. After the selling he is instructed to give to the poor. Nowhere does it say he is to give all to the poor. Jesus has not asked the man to give up his talent of managing money.

Perhaps Jesus recognized that even a great sum of money would not go far and would quickly be dissipated. Remember the parable of the talents in which prudent management of earthly resources is extolled. Also in that parable we have the example of the "Matthew effect "in which he who has great possessions is given even more. Those are Jesus own words. The man is being asked, to give away his identification with material possessions, not necessarily his identity.

As the man is walking away, Jesus says to his disciples how hard it is for a rich man to enter the kingdom of God or heaven. In Mark we are then told that the disciples were amazed at this. Notice what Jesus says next in that version. He says how hard it is to get into the kingdom of God and then uses the familiar camel through the eye of the needle analogy. He is effectively saying that it is hard for anybody, not just the rich. Indeed the disciples then ask the question of who can be saved.

Jesus answer is once again a broad one that indicates that with men it is impossible, but not to the only one Jesus calls good.

Once again it is tempting to be anachronistic and wonder why the disciples seem to be asking a stupid question about why it is hard for a rich man to enter heaven. From their perspective the concept of rich would have implied that such wealth was ordained or blessed by God. If we factor in the ruler aspect, then we have someone who is educated on the best knowledge and wisdom of his time. We would do well not to think that the disciples thought that anyone with money could buy their way into heaven.

The concept of materialism spills over to us to this day for this encounter. We see that the man will have treasure in heaven as some type of delayed gratification in a materialistic fashion. This is rather anthropomorphic in thinking about God and is reminiscent of the essay by Emerson where he says that the common thinking is that we have suffered now while the rich have not but in time will have our reward in heaven while the rich are suffering. When we read the words then you will have treasure in heaven, does it not mean that we will at that moment have the eternal Now of security when we employ our talents for all moments?

We believe that the rich young ruler real life story is meant to read as a parable. We are all the entire rich young ruler with many possessions. Sometimes our possessions are our material possessions. At other times our possessions are our beliefs and our symbols. The question for us today is what are we willing to give up that is not the ultimate manifestation in order to receive the eternal perspective.

Eternal life

For our further discussion of the rich ruler who sought eternal life we turn to the gospel of Mark as our main source. The oldest gospel has the rich ruler running up to meet Jesus. This not only conveys a sense of urgency but also an element of surprise. It is also as though he is trying to catch Jesus off guard. To distract him perhaps in order to get the desired answer to his featured question. He also falls on his knees. Is this sincerity or distraction? He then refers to Jesus as "good teacher". Is this also another distraction?

The final distraction from the rich ruler may well be the way he asks the question "what must I do to inherit eternal life?" Why did the man choose the word inherit. The word inherit almost implies that it is something he is entitled to, unless perhaps he really messes up. Had the man inherited his money and presumed that he could inherit eternal life? Yet the man is perceptive enough to sense that he must actually do something and that is also a key part of his seeking, "what must I do?" So we seem to have this blend of works and grace being asked, whether the rich man perceived it in those terms or not.

Jesus, perhaps sensing both the sincerity as well as the distraction factor responds with his own distraction or turning of the tables. "Why do you call me good, since no one but God alone is good?" He does not give the man a chance to respond before he launches into a listing of key commandments. The ruler then proceeds to note that he was a good little boy literally having kept those commandments since he was a boy.

In Mark the commandments listed were all things to avoid except for the commandment to honor the parents. Ditto for Luke. Matthew adds one additional challenge to love your neighbor as yourself. This good man will be looked at Jesus and have a rare phrase that is rarely uttered on Jesus behalf to another individual. Jesus looked at him and he loved him. Yet Jesus will challenge those whom he loves.

So he says to him to go and sell all that he has and give to the poor. Only then do we find out what Jesus must have sensed all along, namely that the man was not merely rich but that he was distracted by his

Parables and Paradox

possessions. Effectively Jesus has said to the man in the early exchange, you can't distract me with your question or your language, but you have distracted yourself. Now, since you asked me what you need to do, here it is. Go sell everything, give to the poor, the people in Matthew 25, then come and follow me.

Between Criminals

There is some popular theology surrounding the thieves on the cross that Jesus was crucified between. As the story goes there was one on his left side and one on his right. One of them saw the light that Jesus was innocent and asked to be remembered in the kingdom of heaven. Jesus replied that indeed that that individual would be in paradise with Jesus that very night. Of course like most popular theology we wish to choose that which is convenient and expedient for our own tidy understanding while we dismiss without thinking some additional explanations. As an example most people probably do not realize that the story of Jesus crucified between two thieves occurs in all four Gospels. However in only one is there a penitent thief, namely in the Gospel of Luke. In both Matthew and Mark everybody derides Jesus. This includes the crowd, priests, and other religious figures and soldiers as well as the thieves. The gospel of John is rather brief in this regard and only mentions that Jesus was between two thieves on the cross.

Most of us might recall that the Roman official Pilate gave an option to the crowd of whom he should release to go free. In the versions that present the option the crowd chooses the murderer and robber Barabbas. Most of us might recall that Pilate announces that he finds Jesus innocent and seems to wish to release him over the criminal who is also an insurrectionist. If however, most of us were to be asked who it was that named Jesus as the Christ while he was on the cross we would probably not come up with the correct answer. We cannot really count the answer by the centurion who said that this man was the son of God after his death. We cannot count if statements by the rulers who asked if this is the Christ the son of God then let him save himself.

However of the two thieves that Jesus was hung between it was the forgotten thief who seems to identify Jesus as the Christ. That man represents us as we wish to be saved along with what we understand as our religion. That's not how the story really goes though in that that thief was not justified. Rather it was the other thief who was compassionate. That second thief was like the official Pilate in that he could not find anything wrong that Jesus had done but he also practices compassion. In so doing here fulfills the parable of the sheep and goats found in Matthew chapter 25. In this situation the just do their good deeds without recognizing who they are doing them to.

The mission of Jesus begins when a relative of his named John the Baptist is thrown in prison as a criminal and ultimately loses his life. It is a criminal who practices compassion at the end of Jesus earthly life who does not even recognize Jesus like the other criminal does. This is the message of the gospel and how we are to be compassionate to the least of these fellow human beings.

A Wide Net

Arguably the gospel is a wide net cast for many and all who are willing to hear the good news and share love and forgiveness. The gospel is both good news and confrontational as we see in the Gospel of John in particular. These measures will come together in the first meeting Jesus has with the disciples after his death.

The disciples have been living in fear behind closed doors. Jesus will present himself to them offering them peace. This is followed by a gift of the Holy Spirit. This in turn is followed by the charge and ability to forgive. This charge would seem to be a very fitting conclusion to the gospel of John but such is not the case. Nor is it even the final encounter with the disciples.

Rather the final encounter seems to be either a rather trivial encounter with the disciples while they are fishing or one final chance for a miracle. In chapter 21 of John the disciples have been fishing all night and have not caught anything. Jesus simply has them redirect where they are casting their net and there is instant success.

This story represents the completion of the other gospels disclosure that Jesus will make the disciples fishers of men and mankind. Too often time's traditional churches miss not only the boat but the fish because they are not willing to redefine their mission according to the master's direction.

Women

CHAPTER 7

Healing Women

The parable of the unjust judge found in Luke chapter 18 seems to set the tone for how Jesus approaches several of his healings and interactions with women. In the parable there is a poor widow woman who goes to the judge day and night to plead her cause. However he will have nothing to do with her. She however is relentless and will not give up until she gets her justice. Finally the judge says that he does not care about the woman or her cause but he will give her what he wants in order to avoid being bothered by her further.

Some people may be offended that Jesus was comparing his own father God to the unjust judge. What he was really doing of course was setting the tone and standard for how hard we sometimes need to work and be persistent. In particular we believe that Jesus wanted to show a higher standard for females but he recognized that they were going to have to work harder then men in order to receive their reward.

One of the classic examples that Jesus illustrated in real life is found in Luke chapter 8 starting with verse 40. In this stretch Jesus has been summoned by a ruler in order to heal his daughter. The set up here is Jesus responding to a rich male figure. A poor woman who has suffered with a bleeding disorder for 12 years tries to get close enough to simply touch Jesus coat. With the crowd pressing in on him she sneaks up and secretly touches his coat and is instantly healed. Jesus turns around and asks very pointedly who touched him knowing that power had gone out from his body. When the woman is called out about the healing she comes trembling before Jesus only to ultimately be reassured and told to go in peace.

Perhaps a more dramatic example occurs in Matthew chapter 15 beginning with verse 21. There Jesus is solicited by a foreign woman crying out to have mercy on her. Jesus ignores her. His disciples meanwhile, wish for Jesus to send the woman away, but he does not. Instead he challenges this lonely foreign woman that she was not part of his mission. The woman does not seem to care what the original mission may have been. She simply replies "Lord help me". He then gives her a further challenge noting that it is not right to take the children's bread and toss it to their dogs. She has a quick and clever response and knows that even the dogs eat the crumbs that fall from their masters table. (NIV). Ultimately we have a poor foreign female who helps to define and even re-define the mission of Jesus by expanding it to foreigners as well as women. The harshness of Jesus testing of this woman was a reality of the challenges that both women and foreigners of the time were going to face.

True Healing

Before leaving these two miracles of healing, we might ask the question of where does true healing originate. The combination seems to be one of some true internal scene of faith such as the Mustard seed that Jesus talked about combined with a true source of healing, namely in this case Jesus. In the story of the woman with the hemorrhage we have an additional indictment in the version we found in Mark chapter 5. In the new international version we read "she had suffered a great deal under the care of many doctors and had spent all that she had, yet instead of getting better she grew worse." (Mark 5: 26 NIV)

Let us return to another healing of a woman in which she will extend his challenge to the norms of his day with violating two of them at the same time. For this combination of healing return to the story found in Luke chapter 13 verses 10 through 16. In this setting we have the relatively young Jesus in his early 30s doing some teaching in the synagogue which itself would have been unusual for someone that young at that time. This time we do not have mentioned about the woman coming to Jesus but rather simply that she was there and had been crippled by the spirit for 18 years.

In this setting Jesus approaches her and says to her that she is freed from her infirmity and she is healed on the spot. The leader proceeds to remind Jesus rather indignantly that he has violated a healing by doing this on the Sabbath. Jesus then reminds them with a rather practical example of what they would do for their own animals on the Sabbath. He then points out the woman's connection both with Abraham, indicating that this is a Jewish woman on one hand, and the foothold on her well-being by Satan.

Let's turn our attention to other encounters with women by Jesus that do not necessarily involve a physical healing. We have already discussed the interaction with Mary and Martha and the way that he elevates the status of women in that situation.

Another encounter in which she will elevate both the status of women, foreigners, and sinners is the story found in John chapter 4. This is the story of the woman at the well to whom Jesus asks for a drink of water. When the woman points out that she is a Samaritan to whom Jewish people especially men like Jesus tend to avoid interactions with.

Jesus once again points out the original mission of God for the Jews and then surprises her with his awareness of the interaction that she has had with men which is plentiful. This encounter has both measures of direct confrontation and awareness as well as subtleties that may go unnoticed. Jesus accepts this woman with her background and all was without either condoning her sin or condemning it. This combination liberates her to the point that she wishes to tell many others about it even though it will involve a public confession of the challenged life that she has had.

This story is reminiscent of the sinful woman who washed Jesus feet during an important dinner. One of the major importance's of the story is that it is one of the few that is found in all four Gospels. Notably it occurs in Matthew chapter 26 shortly after the judgment day parable in which Jesus commends the righteous who attended people in need regardless of their background. While there has been much speculation and conflation about the background of this woman, we recommend the book Born Of A Woman by John Shelby Spong to further explore this concept.

Finally there is arguably no story that is more poignant than the apocryphal story told at the start of John chapter 8. This is the story about the woman caught in the act of adultery and brought by the Jewish leaders for Jesus two other of his verdict as well. In this drama Jesus turns the table on them and asks that he who is without sin to throw the first stone. After the men have departed one by one, Jesus turns to the Woman and asks where her accusers are. He then proceeds to note that neither does he condemn her but rather that she is to go in peace and sin no more. Spong also has a nice expose about this story as well.

Mary, Martha

Sometimes the gospel can offend us at so many levels if we are open to exploring the possibilities in even the simplest of stories. Take for instance the story of Martha and Mary in Luke chapter 10. Ostensibly it is a very straight forward story in which Mary has chosen to hear the Master and sit at his feet while Martha, as the story goes, is distracted by the preparations. Jesus even chastised her for such it would seem.

First let's deal with our offense. This just doesn't seem fair at any level. Keep in mind it was Martha alone who chose to open her home to Jesus and his retinue. Was it therefore fair for her to expect her sister Mary to assist. Actually, we might still expect it. What we would not expect is for a prominent figure such as Jesus to share openly with a woman as Jesus did with Mary. We might miss the subtle message that Jesus is extending the revelation of the gospel to women as well as men. He is also giving or respecting their freedom and not trying to be that type of Master that controls women.

We might placate ourselves by noting, as Jesus did, that Mary had chosen the better thing and that accordingly we too, should have our priorities straight by taking time to hear and reflect on the words of the Master. We might have the mistaken notion that Jesus feels that Martha should also stop her activities and listen to Jesus as well. Except that nowhere does it say that. Jesus is not chiding Martha about her choice of activities. Rather, he is chiding her about her attitude which is one of worry and upset.

He then notes that only one thing is needed. He does not say that what Mary has chosen is that one thing. Nor does he say that what Martha has chosen is wrong. He says that Mary has chosen something that is better, and that it won't be taken away from her. If we postulate that what Mary has chosen is to be in the moment, this allows for Martha to do her service in the Now moment without worrying how to please or impress, etc.

Washing Jesus Feet

If we are honest with ourselves we sometimes find the paradoxes of the gospels and New Testament and the sayings of Jesus to be offensive. One of these offensive stories is found in all of the gospels making it once again somewhat of a minority, namely a story in which a woman washes the feet of Jesus with a very expensive oil.

The offensive conclusion is basically given in Jesus own words in which he says effectively that in order to love more that we must sin more or at least be bigger sinners.

Let us look at the four Gospels to see what they have in common as well as their differences before we come around to the offensive challenge given above.

First all of the gospels detail that it was a woman who washed the feet of Jesus at a dinner. All of them have in common that someone objected to this use of the expensive oil when the money could have been used for a worthy cause such as feeding the poor. From here our memories may suffer from conflation in which we blend elements of the different Gospels together.

In Matthew, for example, the woman is unnamed and the host is Simon the leper and the disciples are those who complain. In Mark, the most ancient gospel, it is once again an unnamed woman with no specific one named as a complainer but rather a vague reference to "some" while the host again is Simon the leper. In Luke the woman is specified as a sinful woman which is the only gospel to specify that type of background. The host, meanwhile is a Pharisee named Simon, and he is ultimately the one who does the complaining.

Finally in John, the woman is Mary, presumedly the sister of Martha since both Martha and her brother Lazarus who were siblings of Mary were present. The host is unnamed but we may presume that it may well have been Martha because she was the one who was serving. The complainer in that instance was Judas, the disciple who eventually betrayed Jesus.

This common story, as a note, may well give some insight into the angle that each gospel tends to emphasize throughout the rest of that gospel. Only Luke, however, includes the parable within the actual story. In that parable Jesus told a story about two people who owed a money lender some money. One owed a rather large sum which was 10 times as much as the other individual owed. The question Jesus raised to the host was who would love the money lender the most. The Pharisee host answered correctly, according to Jesus, that it would be the individual who owed the highest amount. In fact he uses the phrase that he supposed it would be the one who had the bigger debt forgiven. Jesus next reply shows the wisdom of how he can turn things around with just the right word. Jesus is able to take our supposes as well as our judgments, and turn them into something very positive.

The man may have had a hard time acknowledging the greater love because he had judged the woman prematurely and he issued a weak "I suppose" as his answer. Jesus plays off of that weak answer and proceeds to both acknowledge the woman's many sins, forgive them, and send her on her way in peace. In so doing he does not judge his host for his weaknesses. We would do well to go on the offensive and seek ways to expand our love not by committing additional sins but in forgiving those who have, and send them in peace realizing we don't always know their motives.

Woman Caught in Adultery

The story of the woman caught in the act of adultery at the start of John chapter 8 may be offensive from several different angles. Indeed the original formers of the New Testament were not certain as to whether to include this for perhaps many reasons. It may well be that they were offended by the various measures themselves. They may even have been offended that in this story Jesus allows the woman essentially to go free. Certainly they would not have excluded the story because of its sexual nature. Indeed the Jewish leaders in the story acknowledge reference to the Original Testament principal and law of putting the woman to death.

If we are honest with ourselves, we struggle with where to place the offense in the story. Our first inclination is naturally to be offended at the Jewish leaders who sought to display their brand of justice on this unfortunate woman. The very consideration of bringing such a woman to be condemned before Jesus is despicable. It is indeed a misapplication of justice. We do not need to be any degree of feminist to be offended at the fact that the partner is not brought to the scene. Few people probably appreciate the fact that nowhere in the Bible whether the New Testament or Origial Testament is an adulterous couple put to death. Perhaps the most famous example of such a couple being let off the hook is with David and Bathsheba.

There has been much speculation as to what Jesus wrote in the sand when the question about putting the woman to death was placed to him. Never have we seen any consideration that said "bring me the partner" and then we can talk justice. For the record, we do not have any evidence that Jesus ever finished what he was writing in the sand, only that he began to write. Perhaps we are offended at those leaders because they interrupted him while he was writing and so we will never know those particular words of Jesus.

What we do sense, is that it is not natural to be offended at the woman whatever her actual actions and intent may have been. It does not even remotely dawn on most of us to be offended that Jesus actually never condemned the woman or even her actions. Furthermore we may be troubled in that Jesus did not say that her action was actually a sin even, but only to go and sin no more. Even deeper in the recesses of our minds is the trouble that we sense when we recognize that Jesus did not officially forgive her. Why was this?

Jesus Solicits a Woman of Ill Repute

Probably the last image that we would ever think of with Jesus is that he would solicit a woman of ill repute. That is exactly what happens in the fourth chapter of the gospel of John. The circumstances include that the disciples were not around and that Jesus himself was tired. Apparently he was thirsty as well as he asked a Samaritan woman for a drink of water while the disciples went into town in order to buy food. This seems a little bit peculiar for the man who made it a reputation for making food multiply out of minimum supplies. Furthermore elsewhere we understand that the disciples basically lived off of the goodwill of the people that they were preaching the gospel of love and forgiveness to. Apparently they did not receive those benefits presumedly in their home country of Israel and now were in the land of Samaria.

Now that we perhaps have drawn you into the story let us see how Jesus was perhaps drawing this woman in even as he was asking her to draw up a glass of water. We are conditioned to believe that Jesus merely wished to make a point of inclusion for both foreigners and women. In order for that to be accomplished there had to be a reference to a symbolic metaphor and a revelation. We must keep in mind that this woman who had known many men could not have known whether or not Jesus was soliciting her as it is possible that her answer in the ninth verse of chapter 4 was in part feeling out the situation.

Whatever her understanding of the question was or the intention behind the water, Jesus then references that if the woman knew who is asking for the water that she herself would have asked Jesus to give a living water. While the woman seems stuck on the literal interpretation because Jesus has nothing to draw of the water with, she does seem open to recognize the possibility that Jesus might have something greater to offer then the patriarch Jacob who was the one who established the well to begin with. Note the subtlety that the woman claims Jacob as our father and that Jesus does not make any suggestion otherwise.

This beautiful volley back and forth between the literal and symbolic, between man and woman, between foreigner and native, between person of the world and person beyond this world continues. Jesus points out that anyone who drinks the water from Jacob's well will become thirsty again but not so with the water that he has to offer representing eternal life. The woman now asks Jesus for that symbolic water. Before Jesus will grant that request he tells her to get her husband and come back. Jesus is indeed baiting the woman because he knows that the man she's living with is not her husband and that additionally she has had five husbands before him.

Now the woman is exposed and she proceeds to expose Jesus as a prophet. She then proceeds to do what any of us would do under the circumstances of being exposed for what we are which is to divert the conversation. She chooses the topic of religion and worship and cites the difference between the Jews and the Samaritans. Jesus then gives the recognized differences between the two approaches but points to a time coming when the true worshipers worship in spirit and truth which is what God seeks. He then notes that God himself is spirit and that the true worshipers must worship in spirit and truth.

The woman then recognizes that the Messiah will come and explain everything and in her own words everything to us which itself implies inclusion. Jesus then arguably makes the first declaration himself that he is that Messiah. Later we learn that many of the other Samaritans from the town believed in Jesus because of the simple testimony of the woman that Jesus told her everything that she ever did. We might ask why this was so. Did others feel that they too would have their lives revealed and changed? Or did they come because they sensed that the woman was never judged for her past? Either way we sense that they wished to come to feel a part of the inclusion that involved in Jesus own words spirit and truth.

Washing Feet and Giving Thanks, His Mission and the Cost of Discipleship

Thanks is not a word used readily in the gospels. It is not even mentioned in the Lord's Prayer as we have discussed elsewhere. Indeed Jesus uses thanks only 5 times in the span of his ministry. One of these is where he feeds the 5000 people who have come to hear him in the country and stayed for several days despite not eating. What is Jesus thankful for here? He is clearly not thankful that the disciples could scrounge up enough food. Common wisdom is that he is thanking God for providing something, even a small token, that could then be blessed by God. You know the sermon. Give a little and God will bless the rest. Yet isn't Jesus really expressing a thanks that people who followed him for miracles and signs as that story begins in John chapter 6 are staying with him to hear a message that is unconventional and fresh unlike the stale bread that would have been found in the crowd? Recall again that in the Lord's Prayer we are to demand our bread from God before we have it, not to thank him after we get it.

This first story has an element of appreciation for power and presence that is shared in the story of Lazarus in John chapter 11 where he is raised from the dead by Jesus. To recall the story, Jesus had been close to Lazarus and his 2 sisters Mary and Martha. When Mary points out

Parables and Paradox

to Jesus that he could have made a difference earlier, the KJV points out that Jesus groaned. Then the crowd speculates that Jesus could probably have made a difference.

Once again, Jesus groans. Why is Jesus groaning? Is he touched by the moment as reflected in the mention that he weeps? No, we maintain that Jesus is groaning because people want cheap grace without understanding the cost of discipleship. Jesus then has others remove the stone and then precedes to thank God that he has heard him and that he always hears him. Jesus is giving thanks simply for the fact that he has always been heard and is being heard in the Now moment, groans and all.

Next we turn to the time when Jesus is thanking God that someone has heard his message while others clearly rejected it. Here we blend the stories found in Matthew chapter 11 and Luke chapter 10. The Matthew version begins with the disciples of John asking if Jesus is the Messiah or if they should keep looking. Notice that Jesus does not answer them directly but tells them to report what they saw and heard. He then points out that people had a choice basically to hear the good news from a conservative source or a rather liberal source and did not choose either one. Those choices are rejected by many but the story in Luke appears to be an acknowledgement that at least some people chose to receive the new symbolism for truth. Basically God so loved the the world that he gave people choices. After some condemnation for those who chose neither, Jesus thanks God for revealing the truth to those novices not stuck in a traditional limited way of thinking.

Our final story of thanks by Jesus contains 2 thankful expressions occurring near the conclusions of his ministry at the last supper. In this situation Jesus parallels the story of the sinful woman who washed his feet. This re-enactment occurs at the famous last supper depicted by Leonardo Da Vinci. During that supper Jesus gives thanks twice during this episode that occurs right before he is officially betrayed and condemned. What is it that Jesus is giving thanks for? Keep in mind that in the story found in Matthew chapter 26 that Jesus does not give thanks until after they have begun eating. Keep in mind that Jesus is rarely ever recorded as giving thanks elsewhere.

He breaks the bread in symbolic fashion and then hopes at this late stage of the game that the disciples might understand the metaphor that the bread represents his body as opposed to the literal interpretation of something limiting. He is breaking their understanding of what his life has meant and will mean. Then he essentially does the same thing with the cup. Jesus is giving thanks for something that he will shortly ask to be spared of:" if possible, let this cup pass".

Of course, Jesus has uttered elsewhere that with God all things are possible. What is he really giving thanks for and what is he really asking for? Jesus is giving thanks for his mission as he understands it and the opportunity to fulfill it even when others will not understand that mission. He ultimately sacrifices his understanding of his own mission in order to acknowledge that there may be something higher. He is open to breaking his understanding of his divine calling. At the same time that he is open to that symbolic sacrifice, he is giving thanks. He is effectively thanking a God who can take away the inspiration we have perceived from Him in order to receive an even deeper inspiration.

Jesus is giving thanks for his mission as he understands it and the opportunity to fulfill it even when others will not understand that mission. He ultimately sacrifices his understanding of his own mission in order to acknowledge that there may be something higher. He is open to breaking his understanding of his divine calling. At the same time that he is open to that symbolic sacrifice, he is giving thanks. He is effectively thanking a God who can take away the inspiration we have perceived from him in order to receive an even deeper inspiration.

In conclusion we have Jesus expressing thanks that God hears in the Now and is in the present moment. He is thankful that people have been empowered to carry on his mission even when they are spiritual infants. He is thankful that God is not limited to symbols that need to be broken and even reborn.

Women in High and Low Places

This section will attempt to cover stories not previously mentioned in out other features on women. There is no particular cohesion here other than all of the stories support roles for women in unique ways. Let's start with the high places and review the argument for women as disciples. The most telling story comes from Jesus own mouth as he is concluding a confrontational chapter with the religious authorities on healing on the sabbath, healing demon possessed and blind in Matthew chapter 12. With the placing in proper perspective of the law, Jesus has simultaneously demonstrated when it is appropriate to suspend that law or place it in context.

The question arises if there is a setup for the elevation of women. Let's use Matthew as our model for this discourse since that is where the first key example resides. In Matthew we have a series of generic healings to unidentified people that occur after the temptations of Jesus. Then we have the interlude of the Sermon on the Mount. We almost begin to see faces in Matthew chapter 8 when we have first a leper who was healed and then next the son of a centurion. Still nothing really identifiable here. The first full identification for a healing is no less than the mother in law other disciple Peter. A female of course. Jesus is not merely giving sight to the blind, speech to the mute, calmness to the wild and crazy, movement to the paralyzed but recognition to women.

Chapter 12 of Matthew takes this the next step by pointing out the role of women at a level beyond healing. First of all, to silence the attacks of a religious right who sought to control Jesus, we have a reference by Jesus involving people of a non Jewish background who became significant believers. This was no less than the story of Jonah who preached to and converted the men of Nineveh after God had pledged to destroy the city. So much is made of the 3 days in the belly of a huge fish, just as Jesus was going to be in a darkness of similar proportions and beyond. In so doing we may obscure the role of women we believe that this whole section is leading up to. Jesus will reference the Queen of the South as coming to hear the wisdom of Solomon and then note that something greater than Solomon was there.

We have the recognition of the sign of Jonah when arguably the bigger sign there was the foreign believers. We have the Queen of the South with reference to something greater and the obvious answer seems to be Jesus. Yes, but. The next human encounter is with Jesus addressing the crowd while someone tells him that his family of origin is there to see him. He asks a rhetorical question of who his mother and brothers. Then he points to his disciples and says that these are his mother and brothers. He would not have made this statement about women without women being among his disciples. Echoes of this occur in Luke chapter 8 where women were named supporters of the ministry. Jesus is greater than Solomon not simply because of his wisdom but also the action that takes in women as disciples.

Women Uplifted

Jesus liked the example of women such that he had key references and stories built around them. He tells the parable of the leaven with a female perspective to represent how such a small amount of positive change could affect the whole batch. The ten virgins is meant to be a positive example of females doing watchful waiting for the Master. Perhaps one of the hidden gems is in the parable of the lost coins found in Luke chapter 15 right after the more famous one lost sheep out of a 100 and right before the story of the Prodigal. We are meant to hear the role of women in preserving what is important by going out of their way to find and preserve that which they value, which puts them on par with a lowly shepherd looking for the one lost sheep or the Prodigal where the father does not even go looking.

In real life Jesus will challenge women and uplift them at the same time. Take for example the healing of the foreign woman in Matthew chapter 15 and Mark chapter 7. The woman has a possessed daughter and seeks healing. Jesus notes that such is reserved for God's chosen race, the Jews. Jesus chides her and make reference to her race being like dogs. So let's not miss the setup here. Foreigner, woman, daughter with mental illness. Jesus knows if such a woman is going to survive that she has to be tough and tested. No doubt Jesus senses this and realized that his challenges, representing what the woman actually dealt with on a day to day real way, would be recorded for antiquity as a positive message about such.

In the kingdom of heaven, no talent or gift is too small. Once again like the mustard seed or the leaven, a little bit goes a long way. Such is the poor widow's offering cited in Mark chapter 12 and Luke chapter 21. Jesus says that this woman has given more than all the others because they gave out of their abundance and she out of her poverty. Like the woman who touched his garment, women do not need to do much to yield great impact.

From the time Jesus performs his first miracle which is for a woman, (whom he also makes work for the miracle, even though it is his own mother.) until the resurrection where Jesus first appears to a woman, we see the role of women as inextricably bound up with the message of Jesus.

Parable Gender Part 1

In this section we will explore the concept of which gender may have had the biggest influence on the recording of a parable. We acknowledge taking some great liberties in speculation here but believe that many will find the exercise fruitful for their own reflection. In so doing we recognize that there were followers of Jesus who were men as well as followers who were women as is recorded in the scriptures. We also accept the commonly researched and historically supported beliefs that the gospels were not recorded until quite some time after the life and in person teachings of Christ. Therefore oral tradition would have kept these important stories alive. Our method here will be one of dialogue back and forth as to our speculation on which gender was the most likely to have kept the story alive. Basically there will be 4 categories: 1) predominantly transmitted by male influence. 2) predominantly transmitted by female influence. 3) Could have been either. 4) Clear elements of both.

Steve: Let's begin with the Parable of The Growing Seed found in Mark 4:26-29.

Rich: We need to keep in mind that simply because the main character is a male does not mean that the story was kept alive predominantly by men.

Steve: This is true but I think in this case we can agree that this story would have been perpetuated by mostly men. We have a man planting seed which would have been overwhelmingly men in those days. Then like today's sitcom man he sits back and does nothing while the seed grows on its own. Finally he gets active again at harvest time.

Rich: Seems fairly obvious. Let's keep in mind the counterpoint that there is a fair amount of watchful waiting, and patience involved that often reflects the feminine perspective.

Steve: True, and I think females would have also emphasized the constant nurturing of the crops.

Steve: OK. Let's turn to our next parable: The Parable of Two Debtors found in Luke 7:36-50. I like this story because of the poignancy told at a real live event where Jesus is the guest for dinner at a religious leader's house. A woman who has led a sinful life washes the feet of Jesus with perfume and tears while the religious leader looks on in disgust and judgement.

Rich: Here I have to feel that this story was perpetuated by women, and not merely because the main character was a woman.

Steve: I agree. The parable itself though involves only women. However it does not have some of the harsh male overtones about debt that some other parables have.

Rich: Let's look at the parable of the Lamp Under a Bushel found in Matthew 5: 14-15, Mark 4:21-25, Luke 8: 16-18. I like the Sermon on the Mount version in Matthew because it pairs the parable with the Light of the World. As a household metaphor, I have to favor women telling this story.

Steve: I agree. Only Luke mentions gender which he credits to male. Still with the domestic influence was one likely kept alive predominantly by women. It has elements of the hidden in Mark which uncommonly has the most elements for a synoptic story. I think Luke may have wanted the male influence but that the more original story in Mark is a rare version of being longer and expansive. It allows for the exposure and expressions of things previously hidden such as the female perspective.

Rich: Let's look next at the parable of The Good Samaritan. I think this outreach was one of overcoming prejudice. In the story of the parable itself it is about race or ethnicity, but I think women likely latched on to this and felt it applied to their gender as well.

Steve: I agree. Although all the characters are male there is a strong feminine sensitivity. Males of course may be sensitive but I think the context of told live when a lawyer was asking Jesus about who his own neighbor was expanded on by Jesus to be more inclusive. Curiously, we are not told the gender of the men who did the beating of the individual but I can't imagine anyone listening to this who does not think of men and testosterone doing the deed.

Rich: Unfortunately there are certain stereotypes that we can't escape. The elements of making sure that this stranger who dresses the wounds immediately are strongly feminine. Let's not forget the male influence here where the Samaritan hero puts himself in harms way without second thought, much like a traditional male military hero. Testosterone may have it's presumed downside in this story, but it also has its redemption.

Steve: Good point.

Parable Gender Part 2

Steve: The next Parable is the Parable of the Importunate Neighbor Luke 11: 5-8. This seems pretty straightforward. Men might ignore their friends and neighbors for a spell, but women never would.

Rich: Yes but one that it is often compared with, namely the Persistent Widow or Unjust Judge in Luke 18:1-8 seems to very feminine. A woman who knows what she wants and won't give up until she gets it.

Steve: Even more I like the fact that Jesus is using a female figure to confront a male who is supposed to represent God. We all get that Jesus was emphasizing persistence but the audacity to use a female heroine to confront the Godlike symbol. One of those situations probably not fully appreciated then or today. Certainly a 10 on the Richter scale for the times.

Rich: Next we have the parable of the Rich Fool in Luke 12:16-21. Seems to be classic male greed for a story told in response to a question about male inheritance.

Steve: I agree. As we have pointed out elsewhere, he may also have been lazy and presumptive.

Steve: Next we return to the Sermon on the Mount for the parable of the Wise and Foolish Builders found in Matthew 7:24-27 as well as Luke 6:46-49. My initial impression for the times is that it is about construction and told by males according to the builders of the times.

Rich: I agree although women may have appreciated the unmovable aspect. They also would have warned about the shortcut perils.

Rich: Let's look at the parable of New Wine into Old Wineskins in Matthew 9:14-17, Mark 2:18-22, and Luke 5:33-39. The live background is at a banquet which setting Jesus was known to challenge social norms. Accordingly I think women kept this story going.

Steve: I think that is healthy thinking.

Steve: Doesn't seem like much argument for the parable of the Strong Man or Parable of the Burglar in Matthew 12:29, Mark 3:27, and Luke 11: 21-22.

Rich: Seems straightforward. The inner beauty is that Jesus can compare himself to a thief.

Rich: The parable of the Sower seems to play off of traditional male farming and all the things that can go wrong.

Steve: For me this could be a mixture because the seed is sown everywhere indicating inclusion.

Steve: I don't have a good feel for the parable of the Tares or Weeds in Matthew 13:24-30 where the servants were warned to let the weeds grow right along the good seed until harvest so as not to destroy the good.

Rich: Could go either way but a woman would never be comfortable with a bunch of weeds among good plants.

Steve: Yes perhaps this is related to the Parable of the Fig Tree found in Luke 13:6-9. In this parable the main male figure wants to tear down a tree that has not borne fruit. Another voice which I think represents the feminine pleads for one more year to heal itself.

Rich: Let's look at the Parable of the Mustard Seed in Mat 13:31-32, Mark 4:30-32, and Luke 13:18-19 and compare it with the parable of Leaven in Matthew 13:33 and Luke 13:20-21. We have the leaven being traditionally for the female cooking.

Steve: At the same time we have the mustard seed planted likely by males. I think these stories were paired for Jesus to get the attention of both sexes back to back.

Steve: Let's look at the Parable of the Pearl in Matthew 13:45-46 alongside the parable of Hidden Treasure in Matthew 13:44. To me this represents the feminine side depicted in the lost coins story in Luke 15:8-10.

Rich: perhaps much like the parable of Drawing in the Net in Matthew 13: 47-52 which is very proximate to others above. It represents inclusion.

Rich: You know I like to reflect on the cost of discipleship and so will take the lead on the Counting the Cost parable in Luke 1428-33. Seems to be mostly a male perpetuation.

Steve: I agree as the concept of hating family does not seem to be something that would flow out of the feminine aspect.

Parable Gender Part 3

Steve: Let's turn to the parable of the Pharisee and Sinner or Tax Collector in Luke 18:9-14. Seems like this could go either way.

Ultimately male machismo is put in its place and the humble are uplifted. Accordingly I have to favor the feminine.

Rich: Yes, especially since it is paired with the unjust judge parable.

Rich: I think we have a slam dunk for the parable of Vineyard Workers in Matthew 20:1-16. Men could not keep a story extant that has this much work imbalances, etc.

Steve: I agree. This story would have quickly died without women.

Steve: I think the same thing with the parable of the Two Sons in Matthew 21:28-32. The first son when asked by the father said he would not work but actually preceded to do the work whereas the second son said sure on the work but didn't do it.

Rich: If the father couldn't get the second son to move, I say he goes to the wife for help – and gets it.

Rich: The parable of the Wicked Husbandmen in Matthew 21:33-41, Mark 12:1-9, and Luke 20:9-16 seems so harsh as to be nothing less than male vengeance.

Steve: The violent theme is palpable to borrow from the medical jargon.

Steve: The parable of the Great Feast in Matthew 22:1-14 and Luke 14:15-24 serves as the antithesis for women. The invited guests have shunned the wedding and must be taught a lesson.

Rich: Yes, women demonstrate hospitality and reaping the rewards.

Steve: The version in Luke focuses on not choosing the honored seat at the wedding in order to not be embarrassed. Guys would drink such adjustments off while women would never forget it.

Rich: The parable of the Budding Fig Tree found in Matthew 24:32-35, Mark 13:28-31 and Luke 21: 29-33 does not seem to give much clue as to which sex would have kept this alive.

Steve: I agree by itself, but if paired with the barren fig tree we mentioned earlier we see some feminine overtones, but could go either way.

Steve: What about the parable of the Lost Sheep? To me this is part of the triad in Luke chapter 15 about the Lost. This part of the triad of lost seems the top layer of a sandwich where this is the top layer with male influence predominantly.

Rich: Yes and the lost coin for women in the middle with the Prodigal being the bottom layer of the sandwich.

Steve: Yes, as powerful as the Prodigal is, we have no mention of the mother or other feminine perspective.

Rich: The parable of the Unforgiving Servant in Matthew 18:21-35 seems to be another example of male vengeance.

Steve: Yes, what female would have kept alive a story where the entire household paid the price for the male's transgressions.

Steve: the female antithesis of the above seems to be found in the parable of the Unjust Steward in Luke 16:1-13. To me this is a business savvy response that isn't fair in the male world, but is demonstrating the power of negotiation.

Rich: Yes the male world would never reward this before keep the story alive.

Rich: The Rich Man and Lazarus is our next parable found in Luke 16:19-31. This parable illustrates that there comes a time when it is too late to repent. That does not sound like a feminine perspective.

Steve: I agree in general. It is, by the way, the only parable with someone with a name which could be a faint hint of the feminine.

Steve: I think our next parable of the Master and Servant in Luke 17:7-10 could go either way.

Rich: some might misread this anachronistically as female subservience, but that is not really what it is about. It is about subservience to the kingdom.

Rich: The parable of the Door Keeper in Matthew 24:42-51, Mark 13: 34-37, and Luke 12:35-48 seems open to speculation.

Steve: Yes even Peter who was present for the original story wondered who the parable was for. Jesus seems to be implying that it is for everyone.

Steve: Is the parable of the 10 Virgins in Matthew 25: 1-13 automatically feminine?

Rich: While main character gender does not necessarily translate into who kept the story line intact, it does seem to be the case here. There is however the exclusion of the foolish virgins which goes a little against this.

Steve: I think this is all part of an elaborately orchestrated chapter in Matthew 25 where we have the first parable as the feminine. Then we have the parable of the Talents which is predominantly masculine. The conclusion is the parable of the sheep and goats which shares fairly equally elements of both.

Rich: Indeed, with the Talents we have a harsh taskmaster who starts off with an unequal distribution of talents. Then on his return he seems very demanding. Finally he compensates once again in a very unequal manner. Women would not retell that story.

Steve: The chapter concludes with the end times sheep and goats parable. We have here a king who rewards the unsuspecting dispenser of common every day good deeds. The perfect blend really.

Steve: The parable of the shrewd manager seems at first glance to be so full of male double crossing that it would have been kept alive by men. Of course we don't stop with the first look approach.

Rich: Yes, plus in those times would men have perpetuated a story where a man goes against the boss, and then is rewarded for it? This has some collaboration to it that suggests female relationship building. This is "mom" coaching the "dad" before he really messes up.

Steve: To me it makes it a mixed story. The man acknowledges with typical male pride that he is too ashamed to beg. By the same token, how many guys in those days would have said that they were too weak to do a physical occupation.

Rich: Our intentions must reflect our choice, "Which master do I serve"? That choice will reveal our intentions and determine our actions.

Prodigal

CHAPTER 8

Prodigal Disclaimer

Some people will be troubled by our multifaceted approach to the prodigal. Certainly presenting multiple perspectives on the same story is not a convenient read. Indeed several of them are in direct opposition to another perspective which is also presented. This does not lend itself to a cohesive work of consistency that can be followed from any theological perspective. We believe that such is indeed not only the beauty of this parable in particular but also of the gospels in general. Sermons and interpretations which seek to only vilify the older son while forgetting the forthcoming consequences for the prodigal have their place, but it is a limited one. It is the same type of limits that churches and individuals seek to impose on others by convenient theology to explain and justify their own hidden agenda. Such interpretations are ultimately destined to be on the outside looking in.

A Father's Early Pain on Departure

How do we know or sense the pain that the father had on the departure of the prodigal? We don't have to know much about the unusual request for that culture and time. We only have to put ourselves in the father s shoes. Certainly Jesus knew that this was the first identification that his audience of mature religious and pious men would have. He knew their first emotion would be of disappointment or even anger with the prodigal. They would then naturally be pulled into the anger of the older brother. At precisely that encounter of the faithful pious brother with the father the religious leader audience would have to make a decision. Either they continued to identify with the father or they now were the older brother. The abrupt ending that follows was likely a signal that Jesus departed quickly from that scene while they tried to figure out their own identification and identify.

Another contrast that those feeling the usual sentimental response is that of the father's dismay when the son left compared to his inexpressible joy that he felt upon his return. While much has been made about the father running out to meet the prodigal, we must remember that this would not have been possible without the physical and mental initiation by the son.

The Prodigal Comes to His Senses

After the prodigal has sewn his wild oats and is at his low point, we read in Luke 15:17 that "he came to his senses". Following that awareness or epiphany, he makes his mind up to return home, make a confession, and work as a servant. Once again we may be easily and naturally drawn into the sentimentality of the moment and obscure other meanings.

While of course, the coming to ones senses is generally a metaphor, we would do well to consider the literal meaning. The Prodigal had literally been coming to his senses for some time and seeking out their full expression.

First he had heard about sensual pleasure before he departed from home and sought it in all of its ramifications. He saw firsthand the experiences we might call decadent. He felt and tasted love in every sense of the word. He smelled and indulged in the richest sense all of the foods he desired. He had gone in an effort to experience his senses to the fullest and so it is ironic that we are told before his return that he came to his senses.

Perhaps he needed to let his senses come to him. Perhaps he needed to unite his senses or unite them all with himself. Just like the story of Job, which is a tour de force of sensory experience ignited by the olfactory sense, so too the prodigal has a deep experience with the sense of smell that awakens him. He smells the dung of the pigs and then has his epiphany. He realizes that this is indeed a metaphor for him in that his own life has been reduced to feces. Now that he feels that way, he can return home to the place he may have formally thought of as a dump. In reality an inversion has occurred and he realizes that what he once thought was the ultimate sensory experience was devoid of any satisfaction. What was his first sensory experience upon his return? It was the embrace of his father. He had never felt love like this in his life.

Before Coming to His Senses

We should not lose sight of the fact that the prodigal did not come to his senses until he had received the ultimate insult. A good Jewish boy would not be having contact with pigs or hogs. On the one hand maybe that contact represents his overcoming some bias. On the other hand that contact without the opportunity to even get the scraps the hogs ate was the ultimate in your face or salt in the wounds.

One might argue that the Prodigal used as his first sensory experience upon returning the sense of sight. I suspect that the prodigal though had his head down and did not even see the father. Rather, the first sensory experience upon returning was the sense of touch from his father's embrace. He was literally touched, perhaps in a way never previously experienced.

Image Distraction

We have referenced elsewhere how uncharacteristic it was for a Jewish father in that culture to go running regardless of the cause. This may well have been a purposeful distraction. Consider that the returning prodigal is certainly going to be scorned by the community because of his deviations. The father sensing this makes that instantaneous decision to take the scorn upon himself that is going to come his way. Perhaps today's equivalent would be that a gay son is returning home with AIDS and the father effectively announces "hey we're all a little gay and here's how I celebrate my gayness." It offended the local community as much as someone today offends the reptilian mind when they declare a gender change. We realize that putting this in print is going to offend many in traditional churches. That was exactly Jesus point.

Compassion

There are many poignant moments in the prodigal story but probably none more so than when the son has made up his mind to return home in his utter desolation. After we have the acknowledgement of returning to his senses, we have a mini drama tightly packed in 3 verses in Luke 15:18-21. In those 3 verses the prodigal will rehearse his speech about how he has sinned against heaven and the father and is not worthy of being a son but rather a hired servant. On the journey home the father sees the son a long way off. We are told that he is filled with compassion and runs out to meet him. With this unexpected encounter we will see that the father will cut off the well rehearsed speech of the son and make arrangements for the celebration of return.

What is compassion? What in particular is the compassion of the father? What drives that compassion? When did the compassion appear?

First we look to the Oxford English Dictionary and note that compassion is "sympathetic pity and concern for the sufferings or misfortunes of others". This word, like Whitman, contains multitudes. It implies the plural of suffering and misfortune while at the same time showing not just pity but concern. The word derives from the Latin to suffer with. On the one hand, the Father has been suffering with the son even in his absence. This is no doubt part of the meaning. But there appears to be an implication that the father being filled with compassion is also as sudden as the appearance of the prodigal. No doubt the father had his own well rehearsed speech in the unlikely event that the prodigal ever returned home. That speech though, just like that of the prodigal, is preempted by the moment. Preempted by compassion.

The father has, no doubt, been concerned about the prodigal since his departure and supplicating the God of his understanding. Perhaps also filled with some guilt that most any parent would have upon the suboptimal departure of a child, even when the parent has done nothing wrong. This is perhaps coupled with the pity portion of the meaning. The full meaning of the compassion is not felt though until the father has the unexpected appearance seen at a distance. The distance aspect is important because the father cannot sense any contrition on his face or body language, let alone hear the rehearsed speech of the prodigal.

This is where the other aspect of compassion comes in. The sudden infusion of the other portion of compassion precipitates action. The mutual suffering driven by absence and guilt at a distance will be in an instant replaced by shared suffering in the present moment in person.

This is not all sheer joy at a long anticipated or even hoped for reunion. It is shared pity and suffering in the moment. The moment of the embrace defines and completes the suffering and elements of forgiveness all at the same time. In addition it is a moment of transition that signals the end of suffering and the celebration that is called for with the reunion.

Forgiveness is the driving force behind the compassion. Indeed the biggest problem with the older brother may well be that he stands outside of forgiveness. He has no doubt of his own weaknesses for which he senses the need for forgiveness but cannot acknowledge the need. We must not presume that the father exuded all of his compassion at the brief encounter of the welcoming of the prodigal. The father is still filled with compassion when he encounters the older son. Their exchange outside the festivities is not merely a chastisement, but rather an opportunity for the older son to experience the compassion and forgiveness of the father by his own recognition. Our challenge is to be cautious that our own reasonable judgements that we pronounce may sometimes cloud our ability to see the change we ourselves need to make.

Hunger

Both of the sons have an intense hunger. The younger one has an appetite for measures he knows to be considered immoral. Then an actual hunger drives his goal to return home. The lesson in our own lives of the benefits of hardship may be obscured by our identification with the prodigal over our lusts. We may feel obliged to confess our lusts as he does, but we do not wish to acknowledge the necessary hardships of life that have us asking family for assistance. Especially if we have wronged those family members.

But the older son, though faithful and pious also has a hunger that has not been satisfied. His hunger is almost as palpable as his brother's.

But what is that hunger? Was it love or the lack of perception of love from the father. We don't have any evidence of that. We do have some evidence of lack of self acceptance. He did accept his own resources or position as a son, especially a son with a large inheritance. He did not accept that his father could retain a sustained love over time with forgiveness.

Entitlement

In a sense the older brother represents entitlement. However it is the already endowed type of entitlement in which the wealthy do not wish to let anything be given to those less fortunate or less deserving. Certainly the prodigal who had squandered his share on prostitutes and riotous living was undeserving of anything more. The faithful pious son was not about to endorse a welfare state. We must keep in mind though what is often overlooked. That is we are told that he already had his share as well. There was no proposal to take it back. All versions are quite clear in this regard. Of course the younger brother will serve as a convenient backdrop for someone who represents the failure of the entitlement welfare state who quickly squandered what portion was given to him without doing any work.

The Robe

When the Prodigal has returned in his penitent state there is both profound joy and a sense of urgency as well as over the top sense of celebration. These come together in the fetching of the festive robe. The Prodigal's confession is interrupted by the statement from the father to his servants "Quick! Bring the best robe and put it on him." Then this is followed with the ring and sandals. Why the urgency and why the extremes of show? Is the father worried that the Prodigal might leave again if there is not an urgent celebration that is extreme in its manifestation? Is he worried that the Prodigal might tell him things he does not want to hear? Is he worried that others might hear stories that defame the family name?

The father notes that the Prodigal was dead and is alive. Was lost and is found. The past tense is summarized was dead, was lost. The present tense is alive, is found. So a celebration is commenced immediately. More present tense. The father has done an incredible feat of acknowledging the depleted past of the Prodigal in exactly 4 words: was dead, was lost. It is not dwelt upon in the present moment, but also those present are to note that the father is going forward with the present moment. As curious as the onlookers and servants and friends and acquaintances may have been to know the past, the father pushes that aside for the celebration of the present.

The faithful and pious older brother hears the celebration and inquires of the servants as to the nature. The servants respond that the father is celebrating because the son is back safe and sound, which language comes to us from the King James Version down to many modern ones. Unharmed in one version. Sound? Unharmed? How does he know? The faithful pious son then emphasizes the past. He has been slaving all these years, he has been faithful, he has never disobeyed. He emphasizes the past of the Prodigal by noting that he squandered property with prostitutes. Now keep in mind that up until this point that we have no indication that the father knew a particular sin of the Prodigal. Just that he was los lost, was dead.

The wisdom of the father is that he returns to the present, without lecturing his faithful son. You are always with me, he says to the faithful pious son. Everything I have is yours. Everything. The ring. The coat. The present moment. Not everything **was** yours. Everything **is** yours. You cannot claim what is yours in the present if you are clinging to your pious past. Go inside and put on the robe Your robe, if you believe in me and the present.

Ownership, or Grace, or Works?

An often overlooked concept in the Prodigal is that when the Prodigal asks for his share of the inheritance is that the older faithful pious brother also received his own share. There does not appear to be any resistance or reluctance in that acceptance. The older faithful brother may indeed continue to work implying that perhaps he wanted to improve his lot in life.

Then the hard working faithful older brother hears music and celebration. The brother inquires what is going on. The faithful older brother does not become upset that people are dancing and celebrating. He only angers himself when he hears that people are celebrating for the return of the Prodigal. Ultimately the faithful pious brother is angry because someone is using his very resources to celebrate who does not deserve them. This is about the rules of fairness

On the one hand, the father has taken possessions that are no longer his such as the fattened calf and the special coat and bestowed them on the wayward son without asking the rightful owner. We would be angry as well. That was Jesus point. There is a distraction that seems to be directed to the religious leaders. But it is really for us. We are troubled about the unfairness. We are the ones protesting the distribution. We are the ones protesting that someone who does not share our values is receiving something that not only do they not deserve, but is actually ours. Ouch

We think we can be fairly certain that the faithful pious brother is not upset because he did not get a chance to show forgiveness or grace first. True grace would rejoice right along somebody else's graciousness.

No, the Prodigal has not only disgraced the family, he has done nothing to earn the position back. That of course is the definition of grace. It is not earned. It must only be accepted.

The Prodigal story stands as the epitome of grace. It is also the antithesis of works that we find in our other most representative parable in Matthew chapter 25, of the sheep and goats. At first glance they seem polar opposites. Grace vs works. Yet the common ground is that neither recipient of the good deeds seem to be the most obvious or most deserving. When we put this in the context that the religious leaders want to exclude that which they do not sanction, then realize that we are those leaders in the Prodigal, it leaves us only one choice. To be inclusive is to celebrate with those who don't exemplify all of our values. It is to share from our abundance to the least of these. The least that look and possibly act like us. Ouch again.

Quick, Safe and Sound

The father interrupts the well rehearsed speech and confession of the Prodigal by instructing the servants to quick, bring the best robe to put on the Prodigal along with a ring and sandals. Quick. Before he tells me something I don't want or don't need to hear. Don't ask, don't tell. Quick. Before anybody else asks questions. Quick. Before his older brother who is very pious and follows all the rules finds out. Quick. Before the Prodigal encounters resistance that leads to another departure. The servants do as they are instructed and the celebration atmosphere catches the attention of the older faithful brother who is working while everyone else is celebrating. The servants explain the situation by using the phrase that the Prodigal has returned safe and sound.

Safe and sound. This phrase was in use before Shakespeare and the King James Bible and indeed comes down to us in many versions unchanged to this day. The phrase safe and sound means that someone has been in danger and has come out of that experience alive or unharmed. Now the father doesn't know that the Prodigal has not been harmed mentally. Perhaps even PTSD. This leaves the only thing he can say for certain as that the Prodigal is alive. When the father says that the Prodigal was dead but now alive, does that mean he had disowned him like some religious communities do? Does it mean that he had given up on him for dead knowing the proclivities of his son in a foreign land? Was it merely metaphorically speaking much the way that Abraham believed a metaphor and was reckoned to him as righteousness?

The father has our attention with the strong metaphor of being dead. Now he can soften the process and make it clear that he is speaking in metaphors. For he follows the first metaphor with the statement that he was lost but now is found. This was calculated but quickly on the spot by the father. He is not taking back the dead metaphor but rather modifying it. Perhaps something like giving people various approaches and options of experiencing the pain that he had experienced. How do we know that this was calculated? The father uses the exact same phrasing at the conclusion of the story when he seeks out the older faithful pious brother who is reluctant to come inside and celebrate. Note by the way, that the father never sought out the Prodigal, but does seek out the older brother. Yet the father will close out the story with the same lines that he used earlier. Your brother the Prodigal was dead and is now alive. He was lost and is found. Found is the phrase that concludes the entire story.

Endless Anger

No doubt most of us have kept in our minds the image of the older faithful brother as being eternally angry. However no version suggests that. Rather, the Living Bible has the father saying that the older pious brother has always been close to him in addition to having access to everything the father owned. We sense the older brother walking away from the last encounter with the Father as upset but the problem is that there simply is no mention of that. This is a subtle message for us in that if we nurse either our own hurt or rehearse the anger that another has expressed in a one time, limited fashion, then we are limiting that individuals ability to effect positive impact in our lives. The Master story teller knows that he does not need to spell out the dangers of addiction to anger or harboring it perpetually.

Once again, though, the language of the father is past tense indicating that they did indeed celebrate the resurrection of the brother." We had to celebrate", as though that event is one time past. He was dead but NOW he is alive. He was lost but NOW he is found. I have emphasized the word now as I feel that such was the distinction that the father wanted to call attention to that difference of what was put behind and the current state of affairs. In so doing the father is not denying that opportunity for the faithful older son to also put the past behind him. The question is do we allow that opportunity?

What's in a Name

Another phenomenon that we experience is the names or terms to describe the older brother. We do not want to identify with him and therefore by implication, the Pharisees. So we distance ourselves from him by seeing him as jealous and resentful and vengeful. But nowhere are those terms used. He is described as angry and to be sure, it is a righteous indignation. But how do we perceive him if we use the other adjectives that we use in our paper and which Jesus uses. Faithful, righteous, loyal, pious. The implication here is that going through the motions is not enough here.

Arguably the older faithful son represents an element that accepts standard dogma without ever challenging it until that branch of truth embraces something outside of itself. The prodigal meanwhile represents an element that has been exposed to other ways of thinking, other symbolism, other beliefs. The father represents not merely forgiveness but tolerance and inclusion. We must not limit our perception of the father as someone who says my way or the highway. Nor is he naive enough to not realize that this son will have some new ways of thinking that will not be erased simply because he is returning home.

Jealousy

A lot has been made of the jealousy, envy, or even resentment in the prodigal story. That of the older brother is almost palpable. But what about the father? Why would he not be jealous? Perhaps unlike our earlier discussion, he had not sewn his wild oats, but had always wondered what it would be like to have done so. He runs to meet the youth of experience in the same way that some of us of a seemingly more mature generation embrace ideas or music or whatever of the younger generation. Perhaps he even anticipated that the older brother might see the prodigal first and actually welcome him back but chew him out in a way such as older brothers may that would discourage the prodigal from relating his story.

Perhaps the father knew that the older, faithful brother would be envious and that the father was purposely fueling the fire in order to get him to awaken from his dogmatic slumber. The older pious brother had, after all, shown no signs of growth during all of the absence of the Prodigal. Accordingly, he is much like the rich man in the parable of the barns who wanted to tear down his barns, build bigger ones, and the sit back and eat, drink, and be merry. In that story it is so easy to condemn the rich man as greedy though the alternative interpretation that his condemnation arises from the fact that he has stopped growing is not immediately obvious. Nor can it be discounted when one realizes that there are probably different levels of interpretation for many parables. Meanwhile if the father provokes the older faithful brother to the superficial exterior values brother, then perhaps growth may occur there as well.

The Confession

Did the prodigal ever make his full confession? If so, to who and when? At first glance we might note that verse 21 of Luke chapter 15 is very clear that the prodigal makes his well rehearsed speech of confession to his father who has run out to meet him. The prodigal acknowledges that he has sinned against heaven as well as the father. This is exactly the speech he made to himself when he was coming to his senses at the point of utter deprivation. He did not get to complete his speech as rehearsed. The missing part was that the prodigal requested to be made like one of the father's hired men.

The father, however cut this part of the speech off. We get the impression that the father did not feel that he needed to hear any more. We think we know the rest of the story. The father grabs his robe, the fatted calf is prepared, and a joyous feast is held that the older brother who has been faithful, refuses to attend.

Alas this confession is not good enough for the older faithful brother. However, it is not good enough for the prodigal himself. His interrupted speech leaves him feeling incomplete and he senses the need to say more. How do we know this? We can debate why he felt the need to confess more but not that he did. After all we read in verse 30 that the older brother was well aware that the prodigal squandered his money on prostitutes. We have no direct evidence that this confession was ever given to the father who had purposely cut off at least some portion of the original confession. Did the prodigal feel like he needed to give a detailed version later to the father? Then did the father tell the older son those details?

We maintain that the prodigal may have recognized that his confession was incomplete and that he recognized that he had sinned not only against heaven and the father, but also against the older brother. Then he completed the confession to the older brother with the details that are such a part of AA and other 12 step programs.

If this is indeed the most plausible way that the older brother knew of the prostitute details, then it makes the account all the more telling when the father confronts the older brother. At least at that moment the older brother could not forgive the younger prodigal who had confessed to him. The father reminds the older son that the older brother still has everything in terms of the possessions. But we hear echoes reminiscent of the rich young man in a real life encounter with Jesus, "one thing you lack......" The older son has it all. Except forgiveness. His brother has spilled out his heart to him, and yet he is unable or unwilling to forgive.

The Suppressed Confession

We are sometimes so familiar with a story that we attribute matters to it and interpret it with events that did not actually occur for certain. Such is the case of the Prodigal when it comes to what he did in a distant country. We are simply told that he squandered his wealth in wild living. Let's be honest in that we read in to that story that he was routinely stone face drunk and whored around with wild woman. Most of us have no doubt heard such presumptuous sermons. The problem is that we are never told that. Maybe he embraced an alternative lifestyle. Does not say. Might have had multiple types of arrangements in which sexual gratification was the answer and not a committed relationship of any type.

We do know that he spent everything. Did he spend it on alcohol or other substance? Did he spend it on women? Did he spend it on other sexual relationships? We really don't know. What we gather is that he felt unfulfilled and felt he could spend his way to happiness. He is the quintessential American. The displaced and dispossessed American. The type of person we are told was the difference in the some presidential elections. Indeed he was not entitled because he longed to be fed "but no one gave him anything."

So with no one giving him anything and with a hunger that greatly exceeded his physical hunger, he returns home to confess and work off both his debts and his sins. This is where the version of the Lord's Prayer succinctly captures the double meaning where it says "Forgive our debts as we forgive our debtors." When he comes to his senses, he rehearses his confession and returns home.

He gets part way through his speech acknowledging that he has sinned and is no longer worthy of being called a son by his father. But he is interrupted by his father who wants to celebrate the return. The actual sin is never disclosed either to us or to the father. The father is saying in effect that this is my son, licentious uncommitted heterosexual, or licentious uncommitted gay, or foolish spendthrift, or otherwise, and I both accept him and forgive him. He does not need the details.

The son has done the only reorientation that he needs to ever do which was to acknowledge irresponsible living and offer his life as a perpetual act of work and redemption. The father says effectively with the fatted calf, a ring on his finger, and the special coat that fathers in the Bible reserve for people like Joseph in the Original Testament that he, the father, will take care of the redemption. Only elder brothers ensconced in their traditions and moral certainties stand opposed to such redemption. Accordingly they remain outside of the reconciliation celebration.

Home

> Home is the place where,
> When you have to go there,
> They have to take you in
> I should have called it
> Something you, somehow, have no need to deserve.

When we read or hear Robert Frost's lines about home, we tend to think of a situation like the prodigal son. We are reminded by such imagery that forgiveness is part of the essential equation of home. No matter where we've been, no matter what we've done, someone waits at the other end to take us in. We sometimes forget the following lines that are coupled with them in which it is defined more basically as something that we don't have to deserve. While that seems to complete the meaning that Frost had in mind, the reality is that there is much more to this than a superficial reading of this poem or the prodigal son renders.

With the time or period in which the poem was written and the prodigal delivered have in common is often obscured. During both of these eras there would have been expectations and house rules for which the returning party was very much expected to follow. There would be no free lunch. There would be an expectation to work and assist the household economy. There would be a schedule to adhere to. There would be expectations that there would be some demonstration or acknowledgement of lessons that have been learned in life. Whether or not there were lectures, there would be an awareness that some type of penitence would be performed. When we contrast those expectations with what we see so much of today, we must make an existential decision.

Because we do not wish to sound judgmental, we assume the default position that both of the errors referred to above were riddled either with innocence or naivety. We do not wish to think of the father and the prodigal son as judgmental, because we ourselves do not wish to appear to be in judgment. We are not sure that that really works.

A Father Pleads

Our image of the connection of the father with each of the 2 sons is perhaps distorted over time. For example, if we were to quiz individuals who were reasonably familiar with the prodigal story and ask them which son the father pleads for or with, we might think that it was the prodigal himself. Look again. At no time do we see the father pleading for the prodigal. He does not plead for him to reconsider asking for the inheritance. He does not plead with him to not depart even if the father could guess the inevitable life of debauchery. He does not send messengers to him to plead for his return.

On the other hand, the father does plead for the elder brother to join the celebration. In fact, it is only this situation that the father goes physically out of his way to go outside of the house where the celebration is to plead with the older brother. He does not go out to chastise the brother whom he knows is not only angry but legitimately angry. The brother expresses his frustration with an added historical perspective. He believes that all of these years he has been working as a slave and following orders and not asking for anything.

In mixing in the slave metaphor the older son is still trying to point out that he really is the only legitimate heir. The slave metaphor is tied into not asking for anything and following orders. Yes of course, that's what slaves do. But in reality he senses differently in that as the only son to not ask for anything as well as to be consistently dutiful, that he deserves more.

Maybe it isn't so much that he feels he deserves more but that the prodigal brother, whom he refuses to acknowledge, deserves less, and even deserves punishment. The older brother is potentially troubled by the perception of lack of justice more than his own inheritance being reduced by the return of the prodigal. After all, when the son references the brother he himself has disowned, he notes that he squandered the father's money. An argument can be made that the estate has grown since the departure of the prodigal and is now actually worth more to the older son than it was before. If such is indeed the situation, then this serves as a warning for those of us who are blessed but wish to see others not share in blessings they don't deserve or have squandered.

Suffering, Compassion, and Reconnection

Much has been made of the father seeing the son while he was a long way off and then running out to meet him with compassion. This homecoming exudes sentimentality. As sermons may go, it is as though the father were waiting with a watchful eye for a day he hoped would come or even more extreme, that he knew would come. If there is anything to this foresight awareness, then it strengthens the case that the father too had sewn his own wild oats and knew what to expect. Additional considerations would include that the father had great vision for many possibilities and that he kept an open mind.

While much is understandably made of the great compassion for the son we must not lose sight of the original meaning. The King James Version uses the term compassion as do several others. But other versions including more modern ones employ the term pity.. of course both terms are related as conveyed by the Oxford English Dictionary which notes that compassion is sympathetic pity and concern for the suffering or misfortunes of others. It comes to us from the old French meaning of feeling pity or to suffer with. This suffering with seems to be too easily obscured by the father cutting off the son's confession and immediately arranging the welcome party.

But in that moment of return, the father suffered with the prodigal. He identified with the suffering portion of the son again perhaps because again, he had his own version of this prodigal experience. Then too is the notion that he shared with the son that he had suffered because his life was not whole without the son.

Free Will and the Prodigal

Free will is a major theme in the Prodigal. Without the concept of free will the son cannot even fathom approaching his father and asking for his inheritance. Furthermore without free will, the son would not have carried on his life of debauchery without being sought out by a concerned father. This distinction is profound when we compare the preliminary parables where the woman of means seeks and finds her coins followed by the lost sheep where the shepherd does the same.

Humans have free will unlike inanimate objects or animals. Free to come and free to go, or as in the case of the Prodigal, free to go and free to return. Lecture free, although we can certainly envision a time when the young prodigal was instructed in the path of righteousness and the consequences of deviation spelled out. Perhaps the father himself had spelled out those consequences, knowing himself from first hand experience.

Indeed we must consider that one remote possibility is that not only did the father have his own experience abroad where he sewed his wild oats but also that he was running out towards the son in order to suppress stories that the son may have heard about The experiences of the father. Another consideration is that the father was going to have a vicarious thrill before anyone else in the family or community world. Against the latter notion though is the suppression of the confession by the son.

For those accustomed to thinking of the father in the story as the heavenly father these latter notions are of course blasphemy. At some level though they are not really categorically different than Jesus comparing his own heavenly father to an unjust judge. At some level they are also not distinctly different then the shock value that Jesus was going for when he opened the story of a son who had it made by virtue of a hard working father and then departing from that home by demanding his inheritance prematurely.

Ultimately free will must at the highest level include the ability to conceive of God in much different ways than we have previously conceived. It allows for new symbols and new metaphors to arise while we either replace the old symbols or interpret them in a different light. The notion of interpreting The prodigal son through the traditional lens of the Christian church has been critiqued nicely in the book Short Stories by Jesus authored by Amy Levine

Surprise

Much is often made in a sentimental fashion of the father running to meet the prodigal as though he scanned the horizon around the clock waiting for that opportune time. But what if the father had no preconceptions of such a return? What if he had no more than a vague hope. We already recognize that it was most uncharacteristic for a Jewish father of such stature to run. What about the possibility that the father was surprised and accordingly got totally out of character by that surprise and did a very peculiar thing? We may well have a hard time with the concept of the father being surprised because he represents God. Can we believe in a God that can be surprised?

Ten Commandments

We turn our attention to just one of the Ten Commandments as it relates to the prodigal story: honor your father and mother. Just how does the prodigal honor his parents? First he begins by believing that the Father has something to offer. As simple as this is, it is primordial to all other outcomes. Next the son honors his father by asking for something. Finally he honors him by humbling himself and returning home. He does this after he has come to his senses. Not the sensual experience that he thought would give lasting pleasure but the sense in his heart of the acceptance of his father and that love.

How can we mimic the prodigal without leaving home? In my essay on the Ten Commandments I note that we honor our parents by selecting their best traits and conversely eliminating their worst. We further honor our parents when we show them a better way to do things which goes far beyond our technological challenges. Perhaps it is by displaying an openness to ideas that they have not fully been exposed to. We extend that honor by respecting their belief systems even when they seem so obviously limited. We honor their symbolism even as we seek new expressions of the essence of Being.

Who is Sought

Much is made of the fact that the father runs to meet the Prodigal while he sees him on the horizon, [returning]after the Prodigal has squandered his fortunes and reputation in riotous living in a foreign land.

Parables and Paradox

The story evokes a sentimental picture in even the most unemotional of us. Yet we often forget the context in which this is told as well as the prelude.

Luke chapter 15 has been called the lost chapter because there are a series of lost items from inanimate objects such as coins, to animals as in the lost sheep, to finally the human dimension in the Prodigal. Some have made note of the fact that we begin with searching for 1 out of 100, then proceed to 1 out of 10, before resorting to 1 out of 1 in the case of the Prodigal. The numbers may be correct, but here's the problem. The father never goes looking for the Prodigal. He does not seek him out.

The start of the chapter and instigation for the series of parables is that Jesus was associating with tax collectors and sinners which led to the religious leaders to question Jesus association with such sinners. So Jesus begins with his first story of 100 sheep where 1 is lost. Such an owner would go out of his way and search diligently and rejoice when the lost creature was found. So too, does a woman get in the concept of seeking out the lost when she seeks a lost coin. So too does she rejoice when she finds the lost coin.

Now turn to the Prodigal to appreciate the beauty of having multiple levels of meaning simultaneously. We are set up for the father to seek out the Prodigal. He does not, however. To be sure he does welcome him home and does rejoice with a major celebration, fattened calf, best robe, ring, and all. Was the father unwilling to seek out the Prodigal? Could he have not sent an envoy or at least trusted servant somewhere along the line to find out how the Prodigal was doing? Isn't that what the first 2 lead in stories are about? Yes. But. But the father believed in free will and that only by allowing the Prodigal to risk and perish could he be faithful to his own conscience.

Yet the father is very much willing to seek out the faithful, pious, older brother. The brother who much like the real life rich young ruler, had kept all the commandments since his youth. The father pleads with the faithful older brother to come in and join the celebration. But the faithful pious son rejects the pleas. He cannot accept something that he does not understand. Something that he cannot control. He cannot accept a different ideology. Furthermore, he cannot understand how a loving and responsible father can accept someone who has expressed such a different ideology. He neither understands forgiveness or accepts inclusivity. We cannot begin to imagine what such would look like to the established, faithful, pious of today.

Prodigal Atonement Part 1

Many are troubled by the seeming appearance that there is no atonement by the youngest son in the story of the prodigal. First it is not clear why atonement needs to be part of some unwritten formula that is imperative and governed by a self appointed dispenser of justice tribunal. Nowhere else do we read in the scriptures that forgiveness must be obtained by merit. Rather we are to perceive that true forgiveness is not attached to some crystal ball vision that the party being forgiven is going to necessarily reconcile all of the wrongs that they have committed. This is arguably part of the consideration that forgiveness may be more powerful or at least a more important force in the universe than even love on occasion. Love and forgiveness may be insolubly linked but they sometimes seem diametrically opposed.

In our own little story of interest two of the three parties seem to be quite apparent as to whether they have love and forgiveness.

The father seems to have both which is readily apparent upon any reading. It is the type of love that gives unconditionally even when it suspects that the gift may not be used according to the parable of the talents. We might assume that the ultimate forgiveness of the father to the prodigal upon his return is unconditional as well. But that would be potentially very misleading. No where are we told that the prodigal will not need to make restitution. Indeed it is a bit disingenuous to presume that the prodigal will not be paying back his debt for a long time. Perhaps even after the death of his father.

It appears equally obvious that the elder brother has neither love nor forgiveness although such would be disingenuous as well. The prodigal left at a time of life when he was filled with impulsivity. He lived out a life compatible with that impulsivity it would appear for quite some time. The elder brother had the natural response to both that history as well as the natural response when the prodigal seems to be so welcomed back with the highest position by the so easily forgiving father. The elder brothers brief response while he stands outside the festivities is also impulsive, indolent, and petty. But to freeze him in that position for perpetuity is equally disingenuous.

Opportunity is presented by the father for the elder brother to come around. Review the last 2 verses of the story. The father notes that the elder son is always with him. This is purposely present tense and not past tense. He adds to the ongoing nature of that present tense by noting that everything that the father has is the elder son's as well. The implication is that it is forever. We distinguish that from the final verse which switches to the past tense in regards to the celebration. We had to celebrate implies that the celebration is over. Now it is time to get on with work. The ongoing work of love. The perpetual work of forgiveness. Both love and forgiveness are hard work. Harder than what either brother had been doing.

Prodigal Atonement Part 2 Justice or Inclusion

Yes, there is a tense that the father uses regarding matters throughout the story. He is constantly living and acting in the present tense, with an eye on both the past and the future. In the early part of the story we have only indirect feedback from him. There is no recorded conversation with the prodigal son. We might think that there was a lecture about what would happen to that son in the future if he left the family dynamic at that station of his life. We might go a dangerous step further and propose that the Father talk about his own past and the mistakes he made in order to persuade the prodigal son not to leave the household at this time. But he appears to do neither.

Rather the man of the Now moment recognizes that a certain time has come for the prodigal to learn some life lessons by experience. The next time we see the father is when the penitent prodigal returns home. The focus once again is on the present tense. It is a present tense with an eye on the past and an eye on the future. The in the moment portion is to bring the best robe, put a ring on his finger, kill the fatted calf, and celebrate. Reflect for a moment on what the best robe would be. It would be the father's own prized robe. Somewhat reminiscent of the coat of Joseph. This is the implied time sharing with the prodigal. The prodigal is in that present moment sharing the coat symbolizing a rich past of the father.

We are mistaken if we think that the coat is the prodigal's to keep. Now the father will recognize briefly the past that must be acknowledged regarding the prodigal. First he notes this prodigal was dead. Obviously he was speaking symbolically, but also somewhat along the lines of certain cultures to this day such as the Amish who might disown an individual who went their own extreme way. He pairs the "was dead "statement with the "is alive "to bring it back to the present. He then softens the dead portion to "was lost "as in the past only to pair it again with the present.

For those who live in the present, life is a celebration. There is no choice when we are divorced from the past and not bound to the nonexistent future except to celebrate.

What follows is an exchange between an elder son who is living in the past about both his own faithfulness as well as the unfaithfulness of the prodigal. He also fears the future in which perhaps the prodigal stains the possession of the gifts of the coat, ring, etc. The elder son refuses to live in the celebration of the present. Rather he reminds his father rather selectively what he has done all these years. The reference of the prodigal as "this son of yours" points out a special distance that the elder has drawn.

He no longer considers himself a brother. It is easy to miss the wisdom of the father and thus of Jesus when we fixate on the attitude of the elder brother. The wisdom of the parable of course is that we were meant to reflect on the older brother and ultimately recognize that the parable was not being told simply to Pharisees as a lesson in which they were the older brother, but rather for us. We too are that elder brother when we apply rules of exclusion and fixate on our own system of retributive justice. The beauty of focusing on the present with the elder brother in the final dialogue by the father does not detract from reality. The older son still owns the coat, ring etc. as we are essentially told that in that final exchange. Accordingly there will need to be atonement. Indeed atonement must happen but will only happen when we embrace those disenfranchised as brothers in the present moment.

Jesus Christ Superstar And The Gospel As Symphony

CHAPTER 9

Jesus Christ Superstar as Both Unorthodox and Paradox

We find it interesting to read what is said about Jesus Christ Superstar after nearly 50 years in production. Two generations have transpired and it is still having an impact. Granted this is not 2 millennium like the original gospel. Yet it is long enough to archive it and embed it as an art form to reckon with long term as opposed to a passing phenomenon.

The original score was like the original Jesus Christ, rejected. That rejection for the play script led to an upbeat musical score that only later became the mega play production. The original play sought to restore the emphasis on humanity. In so doing they humanized Judas to such an extent that realistically we can all if we are honest identify with that portrayal. Some of the reviews referred to Judas like the gospel does as the one who betrayed Jesus Christ.

The reality is that Judas represents that portion of you and me that is subject to the betrayal. Judas asked the practical questions that churches today large and small struggle with of how to get the message out about the gospel while still running a business. Indeed anyone who has ever, like Rich, staged a production of the play knows how easy it is to become wrapped up in the crowd mentality and psychology. Even those who wear the banner of Christianity today face the vicissitudes of life very much unlike the crowd in Jesus day.

Andrew Lloyd Webber and Tim Rice wrote the musical and rock opera Jesus Christ superstar at a time when people were losing awareness of the original story especially as a young crowd. They sensed that infusing energy into a somewhat forgotten story would give additional perspective. The process was well received by the Vatican but begrudgingly accepted by Billy Graham. Graham did acknowledge that if the play served to inspire people to read the original stories, then it was indeed serving God's purpose.

Our own writings to date have reflected much of the same desire to have people reconnect with their original stories and find meaning that is applicable to them today. We have made our own legitimate criticism that we have not offered lots of solutions for the problems of today. Also in the play Jesus Christ Superstar there is not much about the resurrection. Indeed the play focused specifically on the final week of events in the passion week.

For that matter the great production by Bach does not focus on the resurrection. So too do we focus on measures aside from the resurrection. This by no means is meant to diminish the meaning of the resurrection as the church at large has done a fine job of highlighting that. Indeed my own experience in nursing homes suggests that the hymns about the resurrection are still some of the last to be retained in peoples memory and meaning banks.

Jesus Christ Superstar II

So exactly how are we inspired today and what do we do with that inspiration? In our estimation we are inspired by anything that is not antithetical to the gospel. We would hope that such is not heretical to the church, but that should not be the case if we keep in mind the original gospel message. It is one of hope to the downtrodden and forgotten, and the marginalized. We are reminded of the Master's own words that "he who is not against me is for me." Then we don't have to focus on being like everyone else.

We do not need to focus on a creed or a denomination. We are inclusive by not being excluding. Paradoxically being inclusive makes us exclusive. Not that we seek to exclude but that we become exclusive by being in a minority that accepts people where they are and does not exclude them because they don't belong to our denomination, our party, our creed.

This is the meaning of the parable of the sheep and goats in Matthew chapter 25. We don't know who represents Jesus or the flock. What we do know is that when we satisfy the need of those in need that we have effectively satisfied the needs of Jesus. This makes the needs of Jesus as reaching out to heal the needy and marginalized. Isn't that exactly what he did time and again.

Those in power are supposed to feel threatened as was captured in the original gospel and portrayed in Jesus Christ Superstar. This is due to loss of control. Loss of control is the biggest fear of most people. Yet that is the paradox of the gospel. Only by giving up control can we enter the kingdom. Only by denying ourselves can we truly find our unassailable core. Unless a grain of wheat fall to the earth and dies, it nears no fruit. But if it dies, it bears much fruit.

Those who complain that Superstar has no resurrection need to realize that we need to have our own resurrection. In order for that to happen we must sacrifice our own symbols. Our symbols, after all, only bear witness to the ultimate truth, the Eternal. The symbols must never be confused with the Ultimate. As such our symbols cannot by

Parables and Paradox

themselves be considered sacred. They may only point to the sacred. We believe our God understands that sometimes we must immerse ourselves in something radically different from what we have been exposed to in order to have an Epiphany like the Prodigal experienced.

We might even synthesize our 2 main parables of the Prodigal and the sheep and goats. What would that look like? Perhaps the prodigal experienced that people have the same needs in other cultures. Perhaps feeling deprived of life's basics made him have an appreciation for those without such that his older faithful brother could not appreciate. This is where we see the application that he who is forgiven much can love much. There is a resurrection in the Prodigal in that the father noted that the Son was dead and now is alive.

We maintain that the biggest ineptitude of the Church comes when it literalizes that which is meant to be metaphorical and misses the opportunity to die to its own symbols and have a true resurrection. Superstar provided an opportunity to question. We believe the questions allow for resurrection, but not simply of a physical body but by any and all symbols that don't recognize the Ultimate and Eternal in the humblest of creatures. Superstar is unorthodox. Paradoxically it has like any medium the opportunity to transform us into the light of the world that we were commanded to be.

Jesus Christ Superstar III

In order for us to take meaningful action in our lives and have an impact on others it is essential for us to find something that inspires us. We must not think of people of any era as any different. Rather people went out to see Jesus not to see a prophet or necessarily to be healed but rather to be moved or inspired. In that sense the lame man who lied for years by the pool remained lame because he could not be moved into the water in time for the healing. It was only when Jesus moved him or inspired him that he had a true movement, perhaps the first in his life.

The rock opera Jesus Christ superstar was being birthed at the time of the close of the tumultuous 60s and the beginning of the 70s. To be sure we were mired in the premises that perpetuated Vietnam and promoted the foundations for Watergate. Young people wanted to make a difference and they were disturbed by the status quo. Music and demonstrations were a mechanism to put the two together. Even as there was a sense of revolution in the air and the urge to overthrow much of the status quo, young people knew instinctively that they still needed stability even as they sought change. Jesus Christ Superstar offered a new expression of a symbol that had been challenged for perpetuity and yet was revolutionary in his own scope.

When the dimensions of music and theater coalesced with the iconic religious symbol, it was inevitable that people would be challenged, offended, motivated, and ultimately effect change. We must not forget that much of the movement of the 60s begin with or at least was greatly fostered by the folk industry and rock industry. Rock 'n' roll however did not emerge with new symbols but only different expressions of timeless symbols. This literally resurrected many symbols from the depths of obscurity back to a position of reliability.

The criticism of the 60s movement is that it led to a surfeit of protests and perhaps even effected some radical change. However many of the leaders and most of the masses were more about revolution and protest as opposed to an ongoing effort to help the downtrodden in all phases of life. Accordingly many of the movements of the 60s were accompanied by unnecessary violence and fizzled out due to a lack of core values. A window of opportunity existed for the church to capture the energy of these movements of revolution but largely failed due to the failure to appreciate the charge given Matthew chapter 25 regarding the sheep and goats. Rather churches have continued to stagnate themselves on the basis of their version of the Bible, their exclusion of people not oriented to their way of thinking, or not oriented in a way that is convenient for them to control.

The formula is no different for us today people. People long to come home just as the Prodigal came home. They wish to come home to something familiar and yet something they can see in a different light. They are not so much eager to reject the actual symbol but they seek a meaning behind the symbol that speaks to their generation. That meaning necessarily involves interaction with others and being open to the others own interpretation of the ultimate meaning and ultimate expression of their own symbols. It must necessarily incorporate the values espoused in Matthew chapter 25.

Superstar John 19:41

The musical scene and mood at the end of Superstar differs dramatically from the frenetic, angry and mocking atmosphere depicted among the events of Jesus' arrest, trial and crucifixion. Instead we are given music that gives us a sense of harmony, peace, rest, even tranquility. It's a strong melody, it has body, it's smooth, in contrast to the jarring notes of the electric guitars, angry rhetoric and music of everything preceding

Aptly this musical finale is entitled John 19:14 a biblical verse that simply states that Jesus' body was laid in a tomb. The dramatic difference, however, between the finale and everything preceding in Superstar is purposeful. It has to be considering the talents of Andrew Lloyd Webber and Tim Rice. They are helping us make a statement. And that statement is meant to be our unique conclusion that each one of us make when confronted with our first hearing of John 19:41.

Is this a tribute to an innocent man? Is it a simple statement of "it's over"? Is it a statement of grief? Is it meant to make you question the purpose of all the anger, conflict, and injustice that preceded the crucifixion? Is it meant for you to feel an acknowledgment that Jesus is who he said he was?

John 19:41 could be a musical expression of all of Jesus' teaching: do what's right for your family and everyone you meet, worship God sincerely, respect society and government. Understand and work for fairness and equity in your life. Reject a selfish spirit. Keep all emotions and reason in harmony. In Superstar, John 19: 41 expresses the harmony of Jesus' teaching beautifully, especially in contrast to the chaos that precedes it. There is a parallel in Superstar and his reality: Jesus taught us how to live a life of Harmony.

Using music, Superstar has hinted at Christ's unique reality earlier in the play. It happens in the tableau "I don't Know how to Love Him, Mary Magdalene's declaration of her conflict resulting from her encounters with Jesus. The musical setting mood and lyrics are also, like John 19:41, departures from prior moments. She can't identify what's happened to her as a result of her encounters. She believes it's love, but it's not anything like her previous love experiences. And something else: she's been "changed" by her relationship, her words calling and hinting at a real change, nothing superficial or temporary. Her change is at the core of reality, beyond carnal and she knows it.

Even Judas' soliloquy near the end is an affirmation of Jesus' mission. Too late, but an affirmation nonetheless.

There's more to Superstar than a Rock Opera. It points us to question we all have to ask ourselves: is He who He says He is?

Who Saw Jesus First After the Resurrection

Like Superstar, the ambiguity of the gospels allows for speculation regarding the resurrection. For the sake of clarity this topic of who first saw or encountered Jesus after the Resurrection will not include God or angels, etc but will refer only to human beings. Like many of our topics we will include all of the gospel stories while acknowledging their differences. We will also assume that the guards who are mentioned in Matthew are not really to be counted on although their somewhat eyewitness reports had enough credibility to be paid off that this should not be entirely overlooked.

We will turn to the oldest acknowledged gospel of Mark for our first consideration. There a group of three women go to the tomb to anoint Jesus. They did not encounter Jesus there. Rather Jesus appears to Mary Magdalene who had been previously demon possessed. In turn she goes to the disciples to tell them but they are in disbelief. Apparently they did not have a perspective that Jesus could appear after seeming death to a woman with such an affliction.

Matthew who borrows from Mark also adds his own twist. In that version Jesus appears to Mary Magdalene and the other Mary. In both Matthew and Mark there are angels at the tomb who instruct the women to not be afraid. Doesn't work too well in Mark. Not certain if it worked in Matthew but we know that there the soldiers were so afraid that they became like dead men. This is not meant to sound sexist but if Mark had the women trembling, we think petrified male soldiers was meant to scale the fear of the women.

Yet the women did their job in each case despite whatever other emotions that they were experiencing. In the Matthew version Jesus tells them to not be afraid, implying that fear was a natural response under the circumstances. It also implies that Jesus could overcome that fear. In

Mark and Luke we are told that the disciples did not believe the women. Perhaps the women not having the expected fear made them unbelievable. Matthew implies that the disciples believed and acted accordingly.

Luke does not acknowledge a post resurrection encounter by the women with Jesus. Rather it appears that the first encounter was with two men on the road to Emmaus who did not recognize Jesus at the moment but only after he mysteriously vanished. The Luke resurrection story is further complicated by the sudden mention of an appearance by Jesus to Simon. This comes from the Emmaus travelers who themselves say that Simon encountered Peter implying such encounter presaged their own.

On the surface the Luke story seems to be slanted against the women and not only towards men, but Simon Peter in particular. A careful review of Luke might suggest otherwise. Peter is an unbeliever over the women's story in Luke chapter 24. While he runs to the tomb, he finds it empty and leaves in wonder. Perhaps he is rewarded subtly for his efforts. Perhaps it is out of forgiveness to Simon which was the name Jesus called Peter earlier when Jesus was predicting Peter's fall. The resurrection is for the fallen and disbelievers while simultaneously exalting the faithful under-recognized women.

Resurrection Beings

We do not approach the Resurrection story as some apologists do with the notion of reconciling disparate versions. We are not concerned about particulars as much as the common meaning. What we are seeking here is to expose the forensics behind the meanings. As human beings we are designed to speculate that which we cannot fully explain. Indeed, speculation may sometimes be the best glue that holds in cohesion the deeper meaning amidst the varied stories.

Parables and Paradox

Amidst the various gospels there is one common element which they all share. The 4 gospels each have extraneous elements that are not found elsewhere in the gospels. Rather they are introduced here for very unique purposes. The elements that we are speaking of here are the creatures that appear after the resurrection at the tomb. Depending on the gospel, we have either 1 or 2 men or we have either 1 or 2 angels.

The common theme here is that these creatures do not appear in any other obvious role throughout the rest of the gospels. Why their literally sudden appearance now? The seemingly obvious answer is that they are being's superior to humans who serve as a testimony and bridge between man and God. They help to support the fact that the disciples did not steal the body of Jesus. Also, that the women went to the proper tomb. Also, that nothing can resist the power of God.

Well and good. Yet we may posit a more practical consideration momentarily. First let us look at the primordial event as recorded in the oldest acclaimed gospel of Mark. This is certainly the most rudimentary resurrection story as told in Mark chapter 16. In this version, we have the 1 man version who is dressed in white who gives the explanation of why Jesus was not there just as he had predicted. Furthermore, to not be alarmed but for the women present to tell the disciples.

Along that line we have what appears to be amplification of the story. This, we maintain, does not change the essential message. Luke appears to amplify this story to turn the beings in to 2 men. Then Matthew comes along and notes that there is an angel, more specifically, an angel of the Lord. The gospel of John, which is generally recognized as the most recent, notes that there were 2 angels. In each situation the creatures are white or dazzling bright.

This brightness may seem a distraction seemingly referring to the supernatural aspect. Alas, though, despite this bright distraction, in each situation the extraneous creatures serve to point out something very human about Jesus. The solo man in Mark tells the women to see the place where Jesus lay. The solo angel in Matthew serves the same purpose. Luke references the clothes of Jesus without reference from the angels on that. John has one angel at the head of where Jesus lay and the other at the foot.

So, what we have now in all of the gospels is the appearance of dazzling creatures in white. What may be lost upon us is that they appear only two females in all of the gospels. In all four Gospels the women are either afraid or troubled in some way with the encounters of these dazzling figures. In Mark the creatures tell the women to not be afraid. The same In Matthew. In the gospel of John, the women are first troubled and then run back to the disciples and then finally meets the angels while she's crying.

In the Gospel of Mark, the women are given physical evidence of where Jesus had been laid to rest. Once again, the same in Matthew. In the gospel of John, we get more details with two angels one of whom is at the head of where Jesus was laid to rest and the other at the feet. In the Gospel of Luke, the evidence of Jesus clothing is given to Peter but not the women even though they encountered the bright creatures.

We have addressed in our book The Advent Style, how the author of Mark reconciled the original ending of that gospel with the women paralyzed in fear and originally not telling anyone, even though the dazzling creature tried to assuage their fear and admonished them to go tell the disciples. In the synoptic gospels the women indeed go and tell the disciples after instructed by the dazzling figures. In the gospel of John, it is Jesus himself who instructs Mary to tell the disciples.

The Gospel of Matthew gives additional evidence of something else that was buried. There we have the story that the religious authorities went to the governor Pilate requesting in advance a guard for the tomb of Jesus. This included a stone with a seal. These guards who were privy

Parables and Paradox

to the original dazzling figures sudden dramatic appearance froze in fear. Some of them briefly told the truth to those religious leaders and then were bought off. They assured the guards who might have faced their own execution for dereliction of duty, that they would satisfy Pilate. We are not told if that satisfaction would involve more bribery or another twist in the story.

Matthew amplifies the gospel of Mark by making the dazzling man into the dazzling angel of the Lord. Luke, the physician, amplifies Mark by noting 2 dazzling men. The first 2 gospels give very few physical details of Jesus post resurrection as well as a limited appearance. Luke gives several appearances including the road to Emmaus and a separate one to the disciples. There they see the hands and feet of Jesus which would have been injured in the crucifixion.

The gospel of John capitalizes on the physical description of Jesus who showed the doubting Thomas the actual nail wounds in the hands of Jesus and the spear wound in his side. Both Luke and John have Jesus partake of food. With all of these physical reminders of the earthly nature of Jesus including the dazzling creatures who have appeared at the tomb, we return to our original speculation.

What was the role of these figures, be they men or Angels?

Ostensibly that role was to be a witness to the resurrection. To show that the women had the correct tomb. To show that the body of Jesus was not taken, etc. Well and good, but how about some additional considerations?

Whether men or angels they appear to have provided clothing to replace the crucifixion tattered linens that some of the gospels mention was still in the tomb. Did they also provide healing ointments to the wounds of Jesus which were visible to the disciples? What role do these dazzling creatures have for our lives? What modeling do they inspire for our own missions?

Stephen Harrison and Richard Huizinga

Why Do You Seek The Living Among The Dead

In Luke chapter 24 we have the resurrection story through the eyes of women. The women have taken spices to the tomb of Jesus on the first day of the week, very early in the morning. We are told that they had prepared their spices. Being good Jewish women they would not have prepared them on the Sabbath. Given that the Jewish Sabbath begins Friday at sunset, then the women have made their preparations sometime during the day on Friday.

Blending this with Christian tradition, these preparations began sometime on the day Jesus died. Specifically we know that from Luke chapter 23 that Jesus died in the ninth hour after a 3 hour of intense darkness where the sun did not shine. By the Jewish tradition timeline then, the women would have begun their preparations after 3 PM. This did not leave much time for them to return to a common place and make preparations. But they did.

The spices will sit for 36 hours. Jesus will rest in repose for 36 hours. The disciples will sit for even longer. But the women don't sit. They don't sit after the crucifixion as their is no time to waste before dark before their preparations. They don't sit around after the empty tomb. They told everyone. To recap, the women leave early morning on the crucifixion day and will have literally and figuratively the darkest day of their lives. When light returns that day, they have little light to waste.

Fast forward to Easter Sunday when they encounter a dazzling light. Brighter than the breaking dawn. But that light is not Jesus himself. Rather that light points out that Jesus is among the living. It dawns on the enlightened women that Jesus has risen as he said he would. They do not encounter Jesus himself in this gospel, though they do in Matthew. Apparently they do not run back to the disciples in contrast to Peter who runs to the empty tomb.

Parables and Paradox

Peter represents the prototypical disciple who has no clue what has happened when he was merely sitting around. We are told that he, with the other disciples, does not believe the women that Jesus had risen. Nonetheless he runs to the tomb in disbelief. In fact, when he leaves that scene we are told that he was still wondering what had happened. We don't know when Jesus appeared to Peter because it was not apparent then.

We do have the interlude of the road to Emmaus where Jesus appears unassumingly to 2 men. He will ask them questions to which he already knows the answer. Then counter to his own admonition to not call anyone a fool, he calls them foolish. He gives a history of prophecy that points to the suffering that the Christ had to endure. The men enjoin Jesus to join them for dinner. As Jesus breaks bread their eyes are opened.

These men mimic the women and return to Jerusalem to encounter the disciples and relate to them. Curiously they mention that Jesus appeared to Simon though we have no other reference in this gospel to such an encounter. As convenient as it is to assume that somewhere along the line Jesus appeared to Simon Peter, we are not told that Simon here is actually Simon Peter and it is disingenuous to presume such especially since Peter is the name used earlier in the chapter.

We are humans though and we are meant to speculate. We wish to change the traditional natural speculation implied and imagine an angel standing at the doors to our churches. What if the brightest light that we have ever encountered or the brightest light that we can endure would ask the same question "why do you seek the living among the dead?" Would that be a wakeup call for us to make an adjustment to our dead theology?

Stephen Harrison and Richard Huizinga

The Gospel for Modern Times

The rock opera, "Jesus Christ, Superstar," has been a center of controversy ever since its introduction. Most criticism is directed against it protests its irreverence, its vulgarity, its theology, or its lack of plot and realism. Almost everyone associated with religion or with the Arts has had some comment on it. For every bit of criticism, there has been as much said in praise of the opera including the subject of its music, content and message. The point is that among the public, "Superstar" has as many champions as detractors which could indicate that we cannot be followers of the crowd in forming our conclusions regarding any production of JCS.

It seems safe to say that JCS is unorthodox. To approach the sanctity of Jesus in the rock idiom is almost sure to shock people, at least the public who take religion and Christianity more literally. The music and lyrics are a patchwork of rock, folk, and Gilbert & Sullivan, laced with the vernacular of today. The discrepancy between JCS and the King James Version or even the New English Bible almost seems blasphemous. However, if the events pictured in JCS are compared with Biblical accounts, the differences arise because of the secular emphasis of JCS as compared with the faith emphasis of all the Biblical accounts of Jesus and His life.

For example, Judas protesting Jesus' anointment in, "Everything's alright", and Jesus' answer is a fairly direct quote from Matthew 26:3-1. But in JCS, the emphasis is on Mary's response and her desire to soothe Jesus. Jesus' response to Mary as imagined by the authors if the events of 4 BC were to take place today - as if we were there when it was happening and without the benefit of the divine perspective.

Throughout all of JCS, the emphasis is toward the human element of both Jesus and the people closest to Him during the Passion Week. The

Parables and Paradox

Gospels almost exclusively emphasize the divine in Jesus as well as the divine or godly responsibilities of the disciples. The public in Jesus' time is always pictured to show how their acts contribute to the plan of God, but JCS takes these same events and makes an assumption that people then and now, we, are not that much different. From this assumption and with the events surrounding the drama of Christ's crucifixion, we get an opinion of what might have been going through the minds of the people surrounding Jesus. Since the Bible does state that Jesus was fully human as well as God, JCS deals exclusively with the imagined human nature of Jesus in the context of his very human contemporaries.

Much irreverence is portrayed; the chief priests, Herod, the crowd, the Apostles. But such Irreverence is also shown in the Bible. The priests plotted against Him; the crowd praised Him, and then damned Him; the Apostles were concerned about "their kingdom" and the King's court; then Peter Denies Him while the rest run and hide or sleep; Pilate finds no fault but yet has Jesus crucified. Even in the King James Version, this is a pretty motley crew which did nothing to justify sainthood until they were confronted with a risen Lord; at least, the Apostles vindicated themselves.

In JCS the crowd is very much in tune with most crowds today. "Simon Zealots", "Hosanna" and "Moneylenders" points to crowds that are interested in themselves ("Will you touch, will you mend me, Christ"), being on the winning side, or a wave from a famous person. But the crowds today and then can just as easily turn against a personality. Today we use polls, then "Hosannas"; and how much like some reporters today does the crowd sound in "The Arrest"

In "Gethsemane", Jesus exhibits some doubts about His purpose here; but one theological point remains intact. As in the Bible, it is God's will that is being imposed. (Matt, 26:36-46) Jesus acquiesces, even though in the Bible, he asks if this cup can be passed by.

The Voice of Judas comes back in "Superstar" and asks some questions that maybe we all have asked in one way or another:

- Couldn't there have been a better time?
- Was Jesus' death necessary?
- What about other religions: do they have as much to offer?
- What do I do about my doubts?

There is one other criticism that has been posted against JCS: "It does not say anything about the Resurrection or Christ's Divinity". While nothing explicit is stated in the opera, there is a strong implication of at least Jesus[1] 'Divinity in the closing selection, "John Nineteen Forty One". By sheer contrast between the tempo and clamor of all previous selections, this last statement stands out for its beauty and reverence, and by its invoked mood, emphasizing and endorsing Jesus' last statement on the cross.

Although nothing explicit is stated about the Resurrection, this fact should not lead us to discount JCS' significance. Bach's "Passion According to St. Matthew" makes no mention of the Resurrection either, yet it is regarded as one of the most religiously moving musical statements of the Passion. The omission of the Resurrection does not offend in this case because it is traditional in its portrayal while JCS is not. Bach chose to emphasize divinity while "Superstar" chooses to emphasize humanity and implicit divinity. Both, however, are serious attempts to provide insight into the events of the Passion Week and after.

"Superstar" poses many provocative questions—if taken as a serious attempt to portray human feelings at the time of the Crucifixion. Maybe we can learn something about ourselves, too. What reaction would you have if you had been there? Remember, there was a doubting Thomas then as there is now; people still mock each other and God; plots against persons and policies are still legion; there is still treason at every level of life; there are still unjust executions; and, there are still many today who, may not mock Christ, but who still wonder if Jesus is what or who "He said He was".

Then there is the possibility that Superstar was crafted with a serious purpose to draw the modern audience into the Passion Week, putting us there watching, experiencing human reaction in the face of Divine suffering. We can criticize the crowd's and Pilate's portrayals of their actions, but remember that we have the benefit of many centuries of theology establishing Christ's divinity. But not then.

Still, there is one scene when Superstar offers an effective glimpse of Christ's purpose to rescue humanity and that's when Mary puzzles over "I don't know how to love Him". Confused over how to express herself, she owns up to her past, but clearly states that "I've been changed, really changed". It's an assertion that her reality is different, she is not the same person and that Christ, Jesus, is the reason. Her love is strangely different now; it has a different component now and she's working out the effect of the "real" change that has occurred.

Isn't that what happens to all of us when Christ engineers a conversion in our lives? Maybe Jesus Christ Superstar is a retelling of the Gospel for Modern times.

Gospel As A Symphony

An ABC documentary on Christianity summarized the impact of its two main players this way: *Christ wrote a Symphony and Paul taught everyone how to play their part.* This comparison might seem a stretch at first, but on second thought it does make sense. Consider the definition of a symphony- a collection of unrelated elements. In the case of its common use to describe music, it is a collection of thousands of differing notes, many different tempos and many different instruments all joined together, collected in a musical composition. Some of the most notable examples are characterized as Musical Masterpieces.

In the case of Christ's Ministry, the symphony description also applies. From a macro perspective, His purpose was to demonstrate and teach all humanity a way to salvation, to Redemption. The elements or components of his efforts were offered to a variety of differing people and cultures. Those who responded, literally millions from all eras, comprise more differing elements than all the musical symphonies ever written. They are and becoming a collection of people, who became, as a group, a Redemption Masterpiece.

On an individual basis Christ appealed to people with a variety of approaches: parables, sermons, prayers, healing and simple rules for living. The basic formula was a simple one: love the Lord your God with all our heart soul and mind and do unto others as you would have them do unto you. Only good can come from that simple statement which is, in fact, the summary of all the law and the prophets. Living with that precept in your mind and following its life implications will be a realistic guide to good and evil, right and wrong.

But Christ offered much more. He offered living relationships with the Almighty, truly songs for the soul. He offered God's mercy for the sinner, instead of the stringency and futility of the law. He offered a simple and effective prayer life with the model we know as The Lord's Prayer. Christ never directly wrote a book of the Bible even though he was the subject of many of its books. His ministry was focused on providing living, relatable examples of how to live. Those topics have been covered in the "gospels" and the stories of Christ's life, his death and resurrection.

Considering all that's involved with Christ's ministry, it's a Symphony

Paul on the other hand, wrote the bulk of the Bible's New Testament, all of it focused on Christ, the theological and practical implications of His ministry. Paul's epistle to the Romans sets out much of the Theology related to Christ. Others, such as Galatians and the Corinthian epistles deal with church and the details of personal life issues. His letters to Timothy and Titus have much to say about church structure and government. Paul seems to focus on making sure that every Christian "gets it right", whether you're in the pew, a teacher, a pastor, a parent, a child, single or married, gifted or not- "You have a part to play in this Christian symphony and I'm telling you how". Paul, after all, was trained by Christ and references that point in Galatians. He has some authority.

So we end where we started. Christ wrote a Symphony and Paul taught everyone how to play their part. Only one reminder: Keep your eye on the Composer when you're playing your part.

Conclusion

Two Parables as a Gospel Summary

As we have noted elsewhere, we can represent much of the gospel in 2 parables. The first is the much talked about Prodigal which when stripped of its sentimentality, remains impactful if we do not limit its meaning to the familiar. The second is the charge in Matthew 25 regarding the separation of the sheep and goats. In the first story we have someone who is looking to see the world who is received back into the fold by a father who was always on the lookout for his return. In the latter, we have an opportunity to keep an eye out for the many disguises that God uses to allow us to deliver his mission. Both involve awareness of the familiar in not so familiar ways. We don't know when the familiar will return in not so familiar form. We don't recognize that the unfamiliar is same as the familiar and even symbolically represents the Christ. When do we encounter the Christ in his many disguises that he uses to provide us with opportunities to witness?

What makes these two parables so representative is that they express at once a longing for return as well as the sense of doing duty for righteousness sake as opposed to merit or even based on someone's background. Both of these parables are extremely offensive and yet inclusive and provocative at the same time. Universality is recognized in both. In the Prodigal we see the father recognizing that the Prodigal will learn valuable lessons in other cultures. In the sheep and goats, we find that the symbolic Christ is everywhere, even when we least expect him. Try to find another parable whose key message is not represented by these two key parables and you will be hard pressed.

Cost of Discipleship

The cost of discipleship is spelled out in many ways in the gospels. Perhaps no 2 chapters do that better than Mark chapter 9 and Luke chapter 9. The chapters share the story of the transfiguration of Jesus along with several other stories. The transfiguration story also appears in Matthew chapter 17. The transfiguration is a wonderful reminder that even someone like Jesus can be made to look more radiant. The radiance is most clear when it reveals his connection with the past as well as with his future glory. Moses and Elijah represent the past and all that it stands for. As dazzling as this is, though, Jesus does not dwell in the glory days of the past. Nor does he simply wish to show that there will be a glorious future. It is rather a here and now moment. Peter not knowing what to say with all of the rich splendor of the moment, suggests that they build a monument to commemorate the moment. He thinks it needs to be forever consecrated. It is no less than God who follows that statement by Peter that "This IS my beloved son. Listen to him." We do not hear God saying that we should dwell in the past or imagine future glory. Rather we are to listen to the I Am who is the Is of the Eternal Now.

The return from the mountain top is met with the harsh reality that there is illness in the world that is not readily solved, even by believers. We are called to deepen our meditative prayer life in order to be able to deal with the demons of this world. We are told at that moment in the Matthew version that we only need to have the faith of a mustard seed and we can do great things, like move mountains.

In the same chapter we have seen the exclusive story where a select group of disciples witness a glorious moment that connects the past and indicates its importance, we have some moments of inclusivity. In the Mark and Luke versions the transfiguration is followed by the healing of an outcast demon possessed individual. Even those with the most violent demon possessions can be restored and included in the kingdom. This is followed by the statement by Jesus that whoever would be first must be last. We must be humble about the blessings we perceive of the moment no matter how glorious they are.

Then we are instructed to be like little children. Inclusion for those not steeped in a limited and prejudiced past. Finally we have Jesus being inclusive for those who are not against him by pointing out that they are ultimately for him. In Luke we have the cost of discipleship spelled out further in that disciples must forsake the comfort zone of home and family and bury their past. The past is the past of exclusivity. Now is the moment of inclusion In which we are challenged to have a deep prayer life, faith of a child, and acceptance of others attempting to do good works whether in the Master's name as in this chapter or as in the unrecognized presence mentioned in Matthew chapter 25 when believers respond to the needs of the least of the Master's brethren's needs.

Jesus on The Essentials

One of the great paradoxes of the New Testament is the ability of Jesus to put in very simple language a profound and eternal truth that may go not completely appreciated by the modern listener. Sometimes it is the context of the situation that obscure is the full meaning for us. A classic example of this is found in the three synoptic Gospels of Matthew Mark and Luke. The setting is one in which once again Jesus is put to the test by the leaders of his time in a series of questions. In Matthew chapter

22 we have a series of questions by the leaders of the religious community to Jesus. These have to do with the authority of paying taxes and then extending those property rights to the afterlife in regards to marriage.

In the second question the religious leaders pose a ridiculously complex question basically about who would have the property rights to a woman who was married to seven different brothers according to the law of Moses after she was widowed successively by each brother. This was an important property rights issue to the leaders of that time. In a rush to reach the following question we sometimes obscure the importance of this particular question for us today. Jesus was basically pointing out that no woman was going to be the property of any man in the eternal life. Rather people meaning both men and women were going to be like angels. He then makes one of the great I am statements in which he quotes the Original Testament saying "I am" the God of Abraham, the God of Isaac, and the God of Jacob. He is not the God of the dead but of the living ". (NIV Matthew 22:32)

This latter question is eclipsed by the heart of the chapter which occurs with the final question from the leaders when they ask which is the greatest commandment of the law. Perhaps this question was meant to distract Jesus Perhaps it was meant to distract themselves from Jesus cryptic but pointed answer about the afterlife. Perhaps the question was even asked to distract the listener before they perceived Jesus deeper meaning about equality in the afterlife and connecting it with the God of the living as in the here and now. Perhaps we too are distracted by the importance of his answer to the second question.

The final question though is which commandment is the greatest in which Jesus basically summarizes all of the meaning of the Original Testament Commandments while at the same time introducing the heart of the New Testament. In Matthew chapter 22 verse 37 Jesus says very clearly "love the Lord your God with all your heart and with all your soul and with all your mind. This is the first and greatest commandment. And the second is like it, love your neighbor as yourself ". (Matthew 22:37 NIV).

This total commitment to loving God commands all of our resources. Effectively it is impossible. In recognizing this challenge Jesus gave us a practical solution to implement in the here and now. That solution is to love our neighbor as ourselves. In just a few chapters we will find in Matthew chapter 25 just who that neighbor is. It is a fellow human being in need when we least suspect it.

I Am Who I Was

To appreciate this essay, we begin with the scripture that notes that Jesus is the same yesterday and today and tomorrow. With that in mind we extrapolate and recognize that the to be verb tenses are essentially the same. Therefore, what I was is what I am and what I will be. For God there is neither a timeline nor a distinction in these tenses and meanings. Our purpose here is not some linguistic exercise or that of pure logic but of practical purpose to uncover the identity of Jesus.

To unravel this identity, we turn to the last parable given by Jesus in the gospel of Matthew. This occurs in Matthew chapter 25 and seems like some other parables to have a very real feeling. We are talking about the parable of the sheep and goats. To be sure because it discusses the final judgment and occurs right before the final betrayal and crucifixion and subsequent resurrection, some do not include it as a parable. Its poignancy is both its beauty and seeming reality.

Chapter 25 of Matthew begins with the 10 virgins who were preparing to meet the bridegroom. The bridegroom was delayed inordinately and all of the virgins, foolish and wise, fell asleep. There is no suggestion of condemnation for falling asleep. Furthermore, there is no condemnation for the wise virgins not sharing with the foolish virgins. Indeed, this refusal when solicited actually appears to be admonished as a strength in the analogy of being prepared.

The second parable of Matthew chapter 25 is the famous parable of the talents. To be sure it is offensive to our ears because of the uneven distribution of talents. Then too, the harsh judgment given to the poor fellow who didn't have much to begin with and then gets his meager portion extracted, seems stringent. We package all these parables together and make a tidy sermon about being prepared for the second coming and using whatever talent we have judiciously.

So now we have the stage with some harsh outcome parables, and we transition to the nearly real. After all the story of the sheep and goats begins with the phrase when the Son of Man comes in his glory. Doesn't get much more real than that. Yes, this story is the culmination of the parables preceding it in chapter 25. It is the culmination of all parables. No matter what we have thought about all other parables preceding this such that they might have applied more to other people, we can't write ourselves out.

Jesus is revealing his identity to us in this very real-life parable. We must keep in mind the challenge of Mother Theresa to see Jesus in all of his humbled disguises. We may be distracted if we think of Jesus as an unpredictable bridegroom who keeps pure virgins waiting inordinately and a harsh taskmaster who gives discriminately while exacting extremely. He reveals is identity as follows: I was hungry, I was thirsty, I was a stranger, I was naked, I was sick, I was in prison. What he was, he still is. Are we so foolish to miss this and bury our talents during today's opportunity? I Am all those. I Am who I was.

The Offensive Gosepl Matthew 25

The term offensive is steeped in ambiguity. There is the affrontive nature in which we take affront at something said or implied. But there is also the other meaning of going on the offensive as opposed to being passive and accepting the status quo. The 2 are not surprisingly inextricably intertwined. We believe that we are meant to be challenged out of our dogmatic slumber and our inattentive social consciousness to action. In order to get to that point we may have to literally turn things upside down in order to see where we need to be. We are, at the most fundamental level insulted when we are told to turn the other cheek when we have been stricken with blows, be they physical or mental. Yet after we have gotten over our offense, we are to Do unto others as we would have done to ourselves. That is, we are to take our offense and put it Into action. No dwelling on the past. Ultimately this means putting into action something that at first glance does not make sense to us or may even be unnatural.

Ultimately this means putting into action something of good work and stewardship for someone that we cannot in any way, shape, or form see as being done for Christ. This is the meaning behind the charge in Matthew 25:31-46. This is a figurative story that Jesus tells to represent the final judgement. All the nations of the world are gathered together, basically for the final judgement. Jesus is describing how they will be separated just like a shepherd separates the sheep from the goats. Jesus is then very descriptive of this separation based on very simple actions of feeding the hungry, giving drink to the thirsty, taking in strangers, clothing the naked, visiting the sick and in prison. It is noteworthy that those who did such actions respond quizzically of when did they see Jesus as needing any of the above. The simple answer he gives is that when you did it to one of the least of these my brethren, you did it to me.

The implications are broad including that at least some of these people from all of the nations included those who never heard the word of Jesus, but somehow had that message of love in their heart and acted on it. Those who get lost in dogmatic differences about faith and works need to look no further. There is no inherent difference between the two. They are inseparable. They may be distinguished at the denominational level but not at the fundamental level. In the words of Elton Trueblood, "Denominations are ok as long as you don't inhale" (Disciples of Christ national Aasembly, Des Moines, Iowa 1985 as attended to by the author.)

Actions are arguably the only thing in the long run that matters. We may be offended that someone does not behave or believe like we do. We may be offended when someone doesn't even appear to be engaged in an effort to help themselves. We may be even more offended when they are doing measures directly detrimental to their health be it drugs, alcohol, or other lifestyle issues. That is not the point as we don't really know on the grand scheme if such behavior are "logs" or "slivers" in the eye.

It is not for us to judge but rather attend to the most basic of human needs: it is the heart of the social gospel. Along these lines, we tend to perpetuate the downside of the addictions of life over their solutions. For example, for years we have been told that rats will choose cocaine over food sustenance even to the point of demise. This was taken as dogma for years and shown reinforced with the same repeated experiment. Then someone came along and realized that the original experiment may have been skewed because rats are social creatures and those original experiments were done in isolation. When they attempted to replicate them in the more realistic rat community, the peer factor greatly impeded the challenged rats who under that influence more often chose the proper nutritive substance over the cocaine. When we are ready to suspend our own judgments and do what is necessary for life, then we can satisfy the needs of the many disguises of Christ.

Interjection

The following 2 essays are met not merely as teasers for our separate books on the Patriarchs Sometimes the Stars Sometimes the Sand and David and Michelangelo: Heart and Stone. Rather they are includes here to illustrate that what we consider as people of great faith because of their works, would still be limited without unmerited grace. This grace includes a type of forgiveness that is unmerited and not even necessarily even recognized as forgiveness, at least with that term. We often think of Abraham and David as big people doing big things. Our writings and their lives will not diminish this perception.

What we wish to inculcate is first that God uses some very flawed people to establish his own legacy. If flawed people with big flaws can be utilized, then so can you and I. This is the ultimate message of the parable of the end times with the sheep and goats. Here we have the antithesis of little people doing little things to other little people. Yet this has as frat a reward as do Abraham and all of his offspring through David and beyond. We cannot accomplish that without the type of grace that is exuded in the Prodigal. A grace freely given that must be freely accepted. Then we are free to do the work we were called to do when we were given our separate and unique talents.

Righteousness

The New Testament makes much about the connection between the faith of Abraham and the Christian faith. In fact Romans chapter 4 revolves around the statement made in Genesis chapter 15.6 "Abram believed the Lord, and he credited it to him as righteousness. ". Let's look at the context and see what that faith and the implications are. The setting opens with Abram getting a vision from God in which he is told not to fear because God will protect him. In addition he will get a great reward. Abraham minimizes this and basically says what good is all that if he doesn't have an heir to share it with. He notes a mere servant is going to get it all. This is somewhat interesting itself in that Lot was still alive and would seem to be a reasonable family member to receive the family wealth. God interrupts him and corrects him noting that he will have a son to inherit the wealth. God then shows him all the stars and makes a comparison that Abraham's offspring will be like the stars, too many to count. Then we have the Cornerstone statement that Abraham believed and that it was reckoned to him as righteous.

Let's break that down a bit. First, Abraham has the courage to challenge God who promised some pretty good protection along with great material possessions, by noting that this All was for naught if he did not have an heir. How many of us would have that faith to believe that we can basically refuse some pretty substantial blessings from God only because we want something more-and before that something else is on the table. We may be further impressed because Abraham is rather aged at this time but still believes. What is it that he believes? He believes a metaphor. God says that his descendants will be like the stars in the sky- too numerous too count. This of course was not a literal statement by God but a powerful and picturesque metaphor.

God then senses that Abraham needs to have something from his past connected to his future. Verse 7 of Genesis chapter 15 brings the three tenses of past, present and future together. There is the great I Am statement implying the ever present Now. I am the Lord..... Next we see reference to the past..... who brought you out of Ur of the Chaldeans(elsewhere referred to as Babylonia). Finally we see the future reference summarized well in the Living Bible......to give you this land forever.(Try not to miss the subtlety that Abraham, whom we think of as always pastoral, lived in the city of Ur, whereas despite our image of Lot with Sodom and Gomorrah, appeared never to have lived in a city.)

Still, after all this and already have been given great credit for faith, Abraham still needs to have more assurance that the promises will actually come to fruition. He then has another vision but this time sees the great suffering that his descendants will experience. Now we might call this true faith in that he is willing to risk the suffering of future generations in order to have them receive the blessings. How many of us can summons that degree of faith.

All this is well and good for our hero and progenitor. But what happens next. He feels compelled to act on God's behalf by having a relationship with his wife's servant girl in order to fulfill that God promise. We have detailed what happens with that elsewhere. For now we wish to summarize that this one reference of faith begins with Abraham's own experience. It ties past, present, and future together. It uses metaphors. It challenges God. Finally, ultimately the promise of God is not obscured just because a man who did not have a complete road map tried to take matters into his own hands. The implications for Christians are enormous and virtually limitless.

Sacrifice or Skin in the Game

The Original Testament makes a compelling case for the long-standing concept of sacrifice. One of our earliest examples of this comes in the story of Cain and Abel. There in Genesis we get the impression that an animal sacrifice is favored cover that of the plant life or vegetation. This seems to be perpetuated by no less than father Abraham who is first asked to sacrifice his son that he has waited until his advanced age to receive. Then an animal sacrifice will stand in the boy's stead.

We may begin to get a different meaning for sacrifice when we come to the story of King David who is considered a forerunner of the Christ. We turn to the story of the confrontation between the prophet Nathan and David. This encounter is shortly after the Bathsheba affair. Nathan tells a tale of a rich man who stole the only beloved lamb of a poor man and his family. Then he used that lamb to be the main course for a fellow well to do acquaintance.

The enragement of King David is raised at the telling of this story such that he demands justice on the spot. What a poignant moment when Nathan points out that David is the man when he took another man's wife which, of course involved the sacrifice of the woman's husband. Yes, the forerunner of Christ has made a sacrifice of blood, but it was that of his lover's partner. When we hear today the phrase that without the shedding of blood that there is no forgiveness, we are met to be enraged like David was over the contrived story by Nathan.

The symbol that we are after here is skin in the game. All of these stories are meant to demonstrate the importance of having skin in the game. Abel took a risk in securing an animal source. He took the risk of losing a source of energy and sustenance as opposed to a more readily renewable plant or vegetative source. The skin in the game for Abraham was that of his own flesh and blood which had been pledged to him quite some time ago. David, meanwhile has sacrificed his morals by shedding someone else's blood.

We would do well to reflect on how we consider Jesus in all of this sacrifice concept. Indeed much has been made out of this concept of sacrifice of blood as essential for forgiveness of sins and therefore eternal life. The real issue here is that Jesus is demonstrating for us how to put the ultimate skin in the game even when other solutions of power display are available to him as he himself says. The sacrifice is the humility of not employing a power play that might be impressive but would place an undue emphasis on power.

Jesus represents what Abraham symbolizes in the Original Testament. He is sacrificing what is ostensibly his promise and legacy only to achieve something far greater than he can conceive in the moment.. The shedding of blood by David represents a misuse of sacrifice as do those who view the shedding of Jesus blood as the means to salvation. The Jesus sacrifice is like that of Abraham with the added awareness that Jesus knows the outcome which his offspring may not fully appreciate until they apply the type of sacrifices in the story of the sheep and goats told in Matthew chapter 25

Parables Summary Multiple Paths From Bad To Good

While our initial journey led us to seek out 5 parables, perhaps we can summarize the message of the parables and gospels in 2 parables. The Prodigal in Luke chapter 15 and the sheep and goats in Matthew chapter 25 seem to be representative of the heart of the gospel. The sheep and goats parable is the parable of the sower, reaping what you sow. It is the Good Samaritain. It is the Pharisee and the tax collector. It is the parable of the net found in Matthew chapter 13 where the good is ultimately separated out from the bad. It is also representative of the weeds among the wheat in that same chapter. It is the parable of talents and what one ultimately does with them which is also found in that same chapter 25 of Matthew. The mustard seed parable in Matthew chapter 13 is the smallest of good deeds that the sheep do to the least of these representing Christ. The goats are the tenant farmers in Mark chapter 12 who do not treat the master's servants and even the master himself well. It is also the parable of the midnight request that is honored even when it is not convenient.

The Prodigal is the unforgiving servant in Matthew chapter 18. It addresses the unfairness like the Vineyard parable in Matthew chapter 20. It is the 2 sons with different perspectives on doing work found in Matthew chapter 21. It is the great banquet in Matthew chapter 22. In a way it, too, is the parable of the talents. The Prodigal is the new approaches versus the status quo as suggested in the new garments parable told in Mark chapter 2. Of course it is the lost sheep and the lost coin. It also shares a stake in the parable of the Sower. The Prodigal is the rich fool parable told in Luke chapter 12 where the man's soul is required because he cannot appreciate appropriately what is rightfully his. It is the parable of the Pharisee and the tax collector in Luke chapter 18. The Prodigal parable is the older faithful brother seeing a speck of greed in his brother's eye that can only be removed after he removes the log of judgement.

We might even boil down the position that the parable of the sheep and goats comes down to action while the parable of the Prodigal comes down to attitude. Well and good. They both involve judgement, but in a paradoxical fashion. The older faithful brother does stands outside of the inclusion celebration because he judges the Prodigal as unworthy. The sheep in the sheep and goats parable are the celebrants at the judgement day because they did not judge anyone on the basis of their appearance or background.

Grace, Talents, and Works

The parable of the talents is found in Matthew chapter 25 immediately before the story of the sheep and goats. It is also found in Luke chapter 19, a few chapters after the Prodigal. In the case of Matthew it seems a fitting and paradoxical prelude to the story of the sheep and goats. In the case of Luke it seems the antithesis or paradoxical response to the Prodigal even though it is not in immediate juxtaposition.

At first listening to a sequence of these 3 stories we would begin by being offended that the faithful older brother doesn't get fair billing and reward for all the years of hard working service. Then with the parable of the talents we might get offended that there is an unequal distribution of talents right off the bat. This is softened perhaps a bit that each was given to his ability. That only sets us up to question the master's return decisions all the more.

The servant gives the uncontested statement that he knew the master to be harsh and demanding. To which the master replies that if the low end talent guy knew that the master was so demanding, then he should have invested wisely. This is more than unfair. This seems a bit offensive. The master did not leave specific instructions. How are we supposed to know what to do? After all, the master knew that this low end talent guy did not have the ability that the other 2 did. The hard working, take some chances, lot more talent guy gets the share of the low end.

Now we are assuredly deeply offended. So what does Jesus proceed to do. Tell us another offensive story that blends elements of a parable with real life. What a transition! But he is not done. Yes you must work. Yes you must do some good things. But you won't always know yourself who you were doing it for or that you even had a reward coming. Look again at who is being judged and what they are being separated on. All of the nations are being judged together. There is no separation of so called Christian nations or Jewish nations. There is no separation on creed, ethnicity or orientation.

Pretty much the spectrum of human need is covered. There are the hungry, the thirsty, the stranger, those in need of clothing, the sick, and finally those who have done something illegal and are in prison. Did he leave anybody out. Yes, he left those out of the eternal kingdom those who thought they knew they were doing good. Those who thought they knew how to discern who was deserving and who wasn't.

So in sum we have this mysterious God who practices Grace after he has been sought out as in the Prodigal. An overflowing, over the top, we don't get it grace. Then we have this other part that says everybody has enough talent to do the work of the master. Finally we have to realize that yes we need to do some works amidst the lowliest and perhaps most undeserving. Please, God. Did you expect us not to be offended? Or were you trying to offend us into action?

The Grace Debate

For reasons unbeknown to us, the concept of grace vs works never really seems to disappear from church dogma debates. For us the issue is not one or the other, but both and only the right application of both. At first glance the Prodigal is the polar opposite of the sheep and goats parable found in Matthew chapter 25. The Prodigal seems to be about grace and the sheep and goats parable about works. It would appear that we very much need both.

Well and good. Grace, though is not simply about each of us receiving something we somehow didn't deserve, but allowing others to receive something we somehow don't understand. That really is the common theme in both parables. The faithful pious brother does the works but does not believe or practice grace. He is exclusive.

The sheep in Matthew chapter 25 have extended grace through works in ways that they had not calculated. They acted without calculating a reward. They acted without knowing what the recipient of their actions represented. This is grace. To practice nonjudgmental decency regardless of merit. Grace is paradoxically free but at the same time comes with a price. This is the cost of discipleship.

Those who believe the story of the sheep and goats is more than a parable will have to deal with the fact that the righteous are those who visited and accepted the people in prison who did something illegal. Something unconventional. Yet at the same time not so obvious such that many are left legitimately asking the question of when would they have had an opportunity to minister to such. The point here is that we have opportunity to minister to all of God's children but that we won't necessarily have the foresight to identify them as such. Some of their actions will be considered illegal. Some of their actions will be easily condemned by the moral majority.

Grace does not weigh in on that. Grace accepts those willing to humble themselves, like the Prodigal. Grace attempts to redirect the faithful and pious who are misguided in their application of doctrine. Grace calmly reminds the pious that everything that the Father has is theirs already, provided that they practice that grace. Grace is ultimately at some level delivering a service to someone who is undeserving and unrecognizable. This is the challenge of both the ancient and the modern church.

www.ingramcontent.com/pod-product-compliance
Lightning Source LLC
Chambersburg PA
CBHW021423070526
44577CB00001B/39